Liverpool's Involvement with American Slave Trade and Its Impact on Descendants of American Slaves:

A Case for Action

Contents

Topic	Page
Overview and Perspective	3-4
Slavery and Liverpool: " Capital of the Slave Trade"	5-7
A Solution for Repair: ASI Founder and Author Norris Shelton	8-13
Liverpool and its Complicity in American Slavery	14
Understanding Liverpool's Connection to the Slave Trade	15-20
Liverpool: Britain's Main Slaving Port	21-22
Seagoing Vessels Trading from Liverpool to the Coast of Africa (Slave Trade)	23-27
The Triangular Trade: Liverpool and Slavery	28-30
Liverpool's Acknowledged Legacy of Slave Trade	31-33
Book chapters relating to Liverpool and the Slave Trade	34-52
Case Studies	
The Case and Southworth records	53
The Thomas Leyland records	54
The Tuohy papers	55
John Tomlinson	56
Liverpool Mayors During the Slave Trade Period	57-58
Liverpool Street Names: the Slavery Connection	59-64
True Stories of the Horrors of Slavery	
Margaret Garner	66-68
Celia	69-75

Extract from The Capture of a Slaver   76-77

The Hanging of Amy Spain   78-79

The Weeping Time   80-86

Specimens of Advertisements in Public Papers   87-90

Recollections of Slavery by a Runaway Slave   91-93

An Epic Love Story   94-99

Charity Anderson – Ex-Slave   100-102

Liverpool's Involvement with American Slave Trade and Its Impact on Descendants of American Slaves

Fact: During the 18th century Liverpool was Britain's main slaving port. Between 1700 and 1807, ships from Liverpool carried about 1.5 million Africans across the Atlantic in conditions of great cruelty.

Overview and Perspective

As a Son of Liverpool is would be an enduring symbol of our great cities culture and strength to be the first people outside of the United States to accept, in the spirit of humanity, the hand of friendship being offered to us by the Descendants of American Slaves despite the horrors, and our implicitly in it, of the past, to graciously, and humbly, accept this offer and volunteer our assistance in any way we can to this strong, spiritual and unique group.

From slavery through emancipation and now into the 21st Century they are still suffering yet they still offer us their hand of friendship.

Can we refuse to help given our past? History has shown that we have the ability to be devoid of humanity for our fellow man, but I truly believe we have the capability to be better and lead the way for others by our actions.

The Descendants of Slaves are not saying we 'owe', they are asking for our help. I think we do have a moral obligation as individuals and as a community to offer assistance to this newest of ethnic groups who are still in their infancy.

We know they cannot rely on the banks and insurance companies that started on the back of slavery and who are still in existence today, posting profits in the billions and assets in the trillions, but I am sure that they can rely on the people of Liverpool.

I sincerely hope they can.

Does the story of the partnership of the people of Liverpool and the Descendants of American Slaves end here.....?

It doesn't have to, nor should it. Liverpool can and should lead the way.

We can do this by collaborating with American Slaves, Inc. (ASI), an American-based organization that has already begun to set in motion a viable and credible process of intervention and reclamation aimed at enlightening and educating America on the plight and promise of Descendants of American Slaves while creating empowering strategies that will emancipate them from government dependency.

What ASI is attempting to do is honorable, and long overdue. When successful, the program that it has developed and is in the process of implementing will have a dramatic and positive impact not only on America, but to all its Slave Trade collaborators around the world. It can build a sense of equal justice and opportunity in a capitalistic western society. It can benefit Descendants of Slave Trade throughout the western world.

However, ASI faces an uphill battle because it is clearly going against the grain. The changes it seeks involve a psychological, political, and cultural mind shift. It won't be easy. And, it takes funding to make it happen.

I believe that we in Liverpool should work with ASI to generate funds needed to support the ASI project. This project begins the process of addressing an egregious activity in which we were complicit, and whose repercussions continue to have devastating impact not only on Descendants of American Slaves but on western culture as we know it.

There are numerous ways that Liverpool can help. A few that will help make an auspicious start include:

1.   Donate to the setting up of DAS Centres in the US
2.   Fund Raise by Partnering with DAS
3.   Organise and Fund a Speaking Tour of Liverpool with:
    - Norris Shelton – President (DAS)
    - Gerald Higginbotham – Vice President (DAS)
4.   Offer Scholarships for Descendants of American Slaves
5.   Offer Organisational Support and Advice
6.   Publicly offer your Moral Support

This document contains information to support my premise on Liverpool's involvement in Slave Trade. Fair warning: some of the images are quite disturbing. However, imagine how the reality of what the images portray impacted those who suffered these indignities and brutal treatment! Imagine the impact of this reality on the families and descendants of these souls! This is particularly troublesome because this dark reality has never been properly acknowledged either by America or those countries that were complicit in these acts. I am asking my friends and colleagues in Liverpool to step up, and become part of the solution.

Slavery and Liverpool

'Capital of the Slave Trade'

Fact: The first known slave ship to sail from Liverpool was the Liverpool Merchant, which left the port on 3 October 1699 and carried 220 Africans to Barbados.

Liverpool is unique. It has long addressed its dark past in relation to the Atlantic Slave Trade. This is now even more evident with the setting up of the International Museum of Slavery and recognition of all facets of the great cities involvement in what is now widely known, and deservedly so, as 'A Crime Against Humanity'.

For many, apologies and open recognition of slavery and the devastating effects it had on the lives of those enslaved and their descendants over a period of 450 years, appears to be enough, and that this abhorrent chapter in our past should to now be consigned to the history books.

But the Effects of Slavery Still Linger on.

Reparations advocates agree, citing differences in prison populations, bias in the application of capital punishment, disparate childhood mortality rates, unequal access to education and health care, and other ongoing inequalities faced by Descendants of American Slaves in the United States.

One of the main problems they face is that there is no special status that ties the devastation they suffered at the hand of America. The status of "African American" dilutes the impact of any aid that is allegedly for their benefit. Assistance that is proposed for the Descendants of American Slaves (DAS) is usually offered as aid to African Americans which includes all people of color who have immigrated willingly to the United States. Thus funding is diluted to the point where it becomes virtually ineffective to those it was initially intended to help. A designated status that clearly identifies Descendants of American Slaves as a specific group is critical to the process of repairing and making amends for the horrors that were perpetrated on the ancestors of this specific group. It is needed to address the after effects of slavery that continue to plague the nation's infrastructure, with deleterious impacts on this special group – Descendants of American Slaves.

Reparation = Repair.

Descendants of American Slaves are not looking for charity or individual payments. What they are seeking is assistance to help them out of an economic black hole through the creation of programs to train and educate towards a healthier future by partnering with other people and organisations to reach this goal in a totally 'inclusive for all' way.

While opponents of reparations point to the unprecedented wealth of the United States, proponents note that this wealth is not evenly or fairly distributed, and that the systematic exclusion of slaves' descendants from positions of political and economic power, though it may no longer be legally sanctioned, continues to haunt Americans. Racism continues to shape the lives of African-Americans and the Descendants of American Slaves, thus reparations must be directed toward repairing the damage inflicted by slavery and racism to the correct group of people.

Moving Forward, Conquering Shame

In order to move forward, Descendants of American Slaves need to understand their collective past. Separate fact from perception formed by media images and stories. Fill in the blanks in their history.

Then it's time to move forward. To form strategic alliances among those willing to work with them. To learn from those who have succeeded, whatever their race or ethnicity.

Descendants of American Slaves must first learn, from reliable sources, the underlying rationale for their belief structure. Separate truth from fiction. When that happens, Descendants of American Slaves will begin to understand the enormous capabilities that exist among them.

Two things must happen. First we, the descendants of the sponsors of slavery, have to conquer the shame and guilt that is our legacy of slavery. Concurrently, the Descendants of American Slaves have to understand the impact of mental enslavement in order to heal, to release the hostility and fear within them.

Since the descendants of slaves can't pinpoint each individual white person who is descended from slave masters, they reflexively dislike all whites. That's why hostility sometimes gets out of hand and runs amuck. It was members of the white race who degraded their ancestors and caused their racial shame. This shameful degradation was passed on to slave descendants. They see and feel it every day, but because of the systematic way they have been made to forget about history because it has never been accurately told, the Descendants of American Slaves, don't fully understand what they are seeing or what they are feeling. The inherited shame amongst Descendants of American slaves causes them to sense that the dreadful feeling came from something they did wrong.

ASI's founder, Norris Shelton, has a firsthand account not only of the impact of coming of age in America's highly polarized and racially charged environment; he has also experienced what it is like to navigate the nation's unequal economic and justice system as a successful and recognized entrepreneur. Mr. Shelton has written an amazing accounting of what it is like to navigate this system of unwritten (and highly unjust) "rules of the road." He has lived the impact of this "shadow" system that creates and maintains a perpetual under class. All is captured in his book, America's Little Black Book. Even more amazingly, Mr. Norris has created a blueprint on how to begin the process of undoing these wrongs without fanfare or deleterious impact on his country's standing in the world. (Truthfully, his solutions will enhance his country's image around the world). This book is American Slaves Inc. Renaissance Plan: The Next Steps Forward.

Mr. Shelton's series of books, along with the support of Mr. Shelton and the Descendants of American Slaves spokesperson – Dr. Gerald Higginbotham – can help us accomplish the goal of illuminating us on the reality of the impact of Liverpool's contributions to Slave Trade.

Together, ASI and Liverpool can begin the process of conquering the shame and guilt that is *our* legacy of slavery. Together, we can assist in removing the shackles that continue to bind Descendants of American Slaves' full realization of their human potential.

A Solution for Repair

ASI Founder and Author Norris Shelton

In addition to being the founder of ASI and the Descendants of American Slaves organizations, Norris Shelton is the author of a series of books that educate and illuminate readers on living as a Descendant of American Slaves. Others can readily identify with the issues and situations presented in his books. One of his books, however, goes beyond reporting. In American Slaves, Inc. Renaissance Plan: The Next Step Forward he presents insights into the impact of racial injustice on economics, culture, and politics. He also presents a plan that will begin the process of addressing these issues in a way that mitigates the corrosion caused by America's failure to properly handle its slavery heritage.

Two of Mr. Shelton's books provide an in-depth understanding of the impact of slavery on the Descendants of American Slaves, and its impact on America at large. They are the aforementioned American Slaves, Inc. Renaissance Plan and America's Little Black Book.

What follows are the foundational principles of the Descendants of American Slaves organization. I believe that these principles are ideas that the people of Liverpool can endorse and support.

Mission Statement:

To enlighten and educate America on the plight and promise of Descendants of American Slaves while creating empowering strategies that will emancipate them from government dependency.

Objective:

To end unintentional discrimination and dispense justice evenly.

Strategy:

Identify members of the cohort group, establish common ground that enables more strategic communication, build bridges across races and ethnicities that are interested in moving America forward, and support projects aligned with DASI's mission and objectives.

Background:

When the history of a people is not recorded, it can be easily altered for avaricious reasons, or misunderstood by the unknowing and forgotten by the uncaring. When history is recorded inaccurately, it automatically breeds ignorance on an all-inclusive, nationwide scale.

Slavery is a shameful part of American history that is saturated with explosive ignorance; it has left a festering sore in the fabric of America.

Many Americans, not understanding inflammable situations, could care less. Not realizing the heritage of slavery, they would rather forget it ever happened. As new information surfaces, we find that slavery is far too important to be forgotten. It is one of the most significant building blocks in the foundation of our great nation. It is the cornerstone of American commerce, a fact that should never be forgotten.

Correcting the Slave Mentality

(Willie's prediction: The slave mentality will last for 300 years)

(KPE) knowledge, planning and execution.

One word that gatekeepers rely on is "security." This term has "African American" leaders all screwed up. Whites have been waving this word in front of slave descendants ever since the Civil War ended. "African American" leaders assume as long as they keep their heads down, protect what is theirs and don't take chances or make waves, they'll be secure like whites are. This is a misleading notion because whites are being led by astute leaders and whites understand how to follow. Slave descendants aren't being led at all and, having no idea how to follow, they just tag along behind the crowd. Following blindly does not lead to security. Racial pressure is steadily building in America. Slave descendants have started killing each other at an alarming rate, and there is no plan in place how to put an end to this senseless slaughter — except one: the American Slaves, Inc. Renaissance Plan! Descendants of American Slaves must acquire leaders with the intelligence and courage to tell unaware stragglers, who are restless and growing up wild, the truth of why they are behind and then teach them how to catch-up!

Until the Descendants of American Slaves are given accurate information, they will stay lost and confused and, because they are frustrated, they will keep right on killing each other out of frustration. If those who aspire to be leaders of DAS, or those who have already anointed themselves as DAS leaders don't start acting like they've got some sense and accept the only viable plan that outlines how their followers will at least have a chance to catch up to immigrant cultures, no slave descendant can be secure — simply because America can't be secure. At this point, grassroots slave descendant don't even try to be secure. They know from experience that no matter the situation they don't have a chance to win, anyway. They figure "what the hell's the use in even trying." That's the wide ranging attitude among most Descendants of American Slaves — and it's defensible!

In an industrial society that boasts freedom for all, fairness is the mother of security. Racial well-being grows into a healthy product when people work together for a common cause. Security is nurtured with knowledge and cultivated with hope. This means that anything other cultures can do — slave descendants should be able to do too; which in their case is not true. Leaders must study the past to understand what transpired during slavery that stops Descendants of American Slaves from progressing like other cultures progress. Knowledge is the key to cultural development in a moneymaking environment. The rest is planning, hard work and execution but the main ingredient is still hope. ASI repeats: Without hope, there is no honest exertion.

Illuminating the security myth

ASI is breaking new ground so, as we go forward, we must always be keenly aware that we are leading a group of unaware people who are held in a deliberately planned unconscious state and, as Willie Lynch predicted, someday they will awaken. This means we must make haste because, at some point, their eyes will come open and they will see and understand the devastation whites caused to the culture that embodies Descendants of American Slaves. To avoid upheaval in the future, ASI's main job is to make waves today! We must plan ahead so the awakening of the Descendants of American Slave Nation won't be a hostile beginning. That's why ASI has worked hard so many years to come up with the American Slaves Renaissance Plan. It is beneficial to all Americans. It generates love for mankind, hope for the future and respect for all human form. To overcome inertia and move forward in a business setting, slave descendants must keep the six P's of business at the forefront of their way of thinking: "Proper Planning Prevents Piss Poor Performance." Proper planning is the mother of proper execution. America's Little Black Book gives us the key to success: "KPE," (Knowledge, Planning and Execution). If understood, the information in the book will lead slave descendants in the direction of security. It is left to those who have the mettle to lead a group of abandoned slaves to come up with a viable plan and then teach the slave culture how to execute it properly so they can reach their planned goal.

The single most important rule that controls a business society where residing cultures compete is to make money collectively. The culture embedded in the Descendants of American Slaves group is impoverished because, as a people, slaves absolutely refused to work collectively unless whites are in charge. Descendants of Slaves think they are working together, independent of whites, but they are not. The white culture has always been in charge. Their group is affluent because they believe in working together, no matter who's in charge, even if it's a Descendant of American Slaves and the consequences are obvious.

Now that we have explored the problems that slave descendants are faced with, before we move forward, let us look back at what we have to work with: Number one: Slaves were bred in America which was an immoral act sanctioned by white Americans - the dominant culture. Number two: Slavery was a legal business enterprise and recognized as such by America's "powers that be." Number three: Slavery was ultimately judged to be illegal and immoral. That's the chief reason why the Civil War was fought and why white people killed each other — but that's not the full account of human bondage. There are other pieces of the slavery puzzle that must be taken into considerations: America is a commercial society that is controlled by legalities and strict guidelines. Even though the white culture is the dominant culture and can do pretty much whatever it wants to do, its people didn't just wake up one morning and start killing each other because the North hated the South nor because either locale loved slaves. The North and South were involved in fierce economic competition that would shape America for the future. To gain an advantage, the South started mass-breeding slaves right out in the open. Profits from slavery allowed the South to rise in prominence. However, the illegal act of slavery prompted the North to fight the South until they unchained their slaves. That's not the end of the slavery story either; because slave descendants survived and America is still ongoing — therefore, the story continues.

I'm Not Angry; I'm Just Doing Business! (Business mentality acquired)

Testing slave descendants' resolve to do business — American style

The time has finally arrived for slave descendants to rise up, leave stagnation behind and begin to move forward. To advance, leaders must drop their false pride, get their heads together and realize they all have something to offer to the Descendants of American Slave Movement. It's the only way they can take an accurate analysis of slave descendants' collective situation. Once leaders begin collaborating, a starting point can be established and a plan of action that is beneficial to slave descendants and acceptable to commercial America can be devised. It's

important that this plan is supported by the religious sector of both the black and white communities. Subsequent to a plan of action being accepted by a cross-section of the population, it could then be introduced as legislation to support a political agenda for the slave culture (America's Little Black Book, Page 183, subtitle: "Laying the structural foundation").

Those who lead slave descendants must acknowledge that racial ignorance, the toughest roadblock of all, is what has been holding the culture of descendants of slaves back all the time. Acknowledgement is important because racial ignorance is not the same as individual ignorance. Precise steps must be taken to reverse the injected ignorance Descendants of American Slaves inherited because, even though it started at birth and rose to the top, it now flows from the top down. To move a group of abandoned people who are unaware and also have an identity crisis forward, intelligence must be injected into the head of the group directly. This sounds difficult but it's not. All leaders have to do is open their minds and accept logic. An admission of ignorance by "African American" leaders will illustrate their ability to accept intelligence. The next step is to initiate a special educational program that encompasses the culture that envelops descendants of slaves. This is necessary because this group has been made ignorant of their pre-planned cultural existence.

Slave descendants must be singled out so America's education system can target their effort toward providing their teachers and other educators with accurate knowledge according to their group's investigated needs, their recorded stagnation, and anticipated growth. This step must be headed up by an institution of higher learning and carried out by America's education system in general. The next step is to clarify the legalities of slavery. This is the most imperative step in establishing well-being in the slave culture. If carried out properly, it will ensure that slave descendants are legally recognized as an American people in every area that controls cultural advancement.

Prepared For The
St. Louis Regional Chamber
by
American Slaves, Inc.
Clearinghouse Plan

2014
3303 Goodfellow Blvd., St. Louis, MO 63120

314 972-0542

Charitable and minority programs are inadvertently biased disregarding an American bred people. To end unintentional discrimination and dispense justice evenly, charitable and minority organizations must recognize Descendants of American Slaves as an American culture. To insure fair-play, charitable contributions must be awarded without the influence of racial discrimination and obvious exclusion.

Racial intolerance is causing cultural unrest in the heart America. To curb what is fast becoming an epidemic, American Slaves, Inc. drafted the American Slaves Renaissance Plan. To implement the plan, sequential steps must be taken: Descendants of American Slaves must be accurately identified and their proper, identifying name included in the language that governs minority and charitable programs. Accurate identification will enable slave descendants to receive appropriate help, including their fair share of America's affluence and charitable generosity.

Liverpool and its Complicity in American Slavery

As pointed out Mr. Shelton books, slavery was an economic system that greatly benefited America, as well as most of the Western world. His claims are clearly documented in Liverpool's history.   The LIVERPOOL MARITIME ARCHIVES & LIBRARY has an excellent accounting of Liverpool's involvement in slave trade.   There are also numerous additional sources that document Liverpool's activities.

The following pages contain exhibits that provide evidence of Liverpool's complicity.

Understanding Liverpool's Connection to the Slave Trade

This source provides clear insights into the relationship between Liverpool's economics and slave trade. It also affirms that the city of Liverpool now officially acknowledges the fact of it once being a major slaving port with the opening of the International Slavery Museum on 23 August, 2007.

Liverpool's Slave Traders

Between 1700 and 1800, Liverpool was transformed from not much more than a fishing village into one of the busiest slave-trading ports in the world and thence into a general trading port and city without peer in the 19th and 20th Centuries.

An estimated 15 million Africans were transported as slaves to the Americas between 1540 and 1850. Ships from Liverpool accounted for more than 40% of the European slave trade.

The town and its inhabitants derived great wealth from the trade. It laid the foundations for the town's growth. It is no exaggeration to say that the grand buildings which grace Liverpool's waterfront and inner heart today were built with the blood money of slavery.

In order to understand how and why Liverpool flourished in this way, it is necessary to explain something about the nature of the Slave Trade.

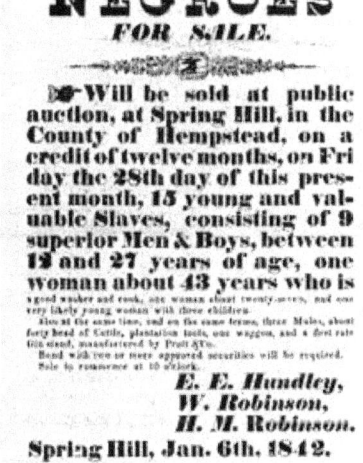

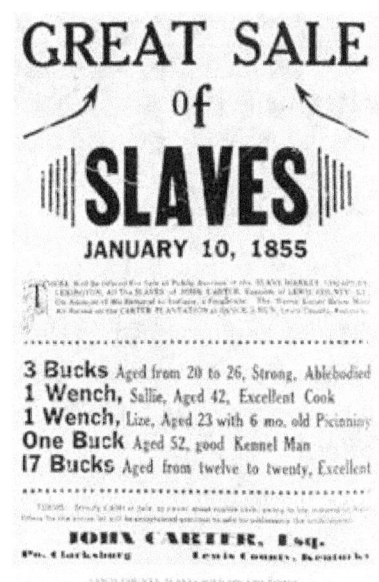

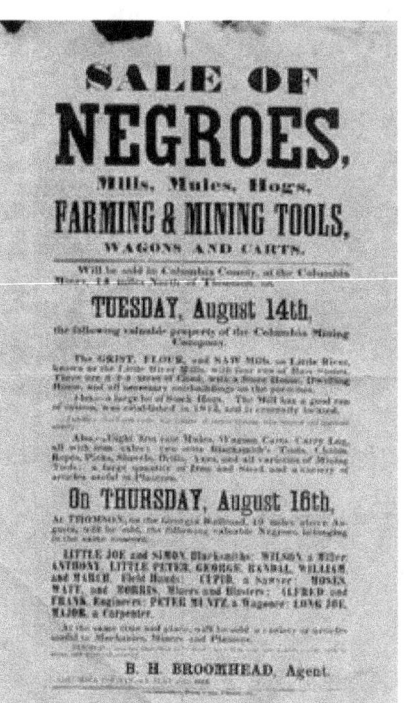

Background to the Slave Trade

After the European discovery of the Americas and West Indies, land was distributed to Europeans who founded plantations to grow commodities much sought after back home. These included sugar, tobacco and cotton. In order to produce goods at a profitable rate, cheap labour was required to work the plantations.

At first, the native people of America and the West Indies were used as slaves but overwork, disease and ill-treatment led to serious labour shortages. Attempts were then made to obtain labour from Ireland and England. English servants could gain free passage and the promise of land, by agreeing to be bound to an employer[1] for a set number of years, but few took up the offer.

Why Slaves From Africa?

Europeans were trading in Africa as well as the New World. Slavery already existed in Africa, where tribes enslaved people from other ethnic groups, as prisoners of war, in payment for debt or as a punishment for crimes. African slaves started to be shipped to the plantations in the Americas. To meet the increasing demand from European traders, there was a marked increase in the numbers of wars, raids and kidnapping of individuals, particularly on the west coast.

Landowners in the Americas quickly concluded that African slaves were more suitable than the English or Irish. The reasons usually stated for African slaves being preferred is that they could easily be bought from traders on the West African coast and were more immune to disease than indigenous Americans or imported white slaves. Although there is some truth in these arguments, the main reason was that Africans made good slave labourers because many of them were skilled artisans.

However the hard life of a slave meant nearly one-third of all slaves dying within three years, creating a constant demand to replace them.

Thus started a notorious period in British and American history: that of the Slave Trade.

The Trade Triangle

The transatlantic slave trade generally followed a triangular route. Traders set out from European ports towards Africa's west coast laden with items such as guns, cloth and metal goods. There they bought slaves in exchange for their European cargo and loaded them into the ships. The voyage across the Atlantic itself generally took six to eight weeks. Once in the Americas, those Africans who had survived the journey were off-loaded for sale and put to work as slaves. The ships returned to Europe with goods such as sugar, coffee, tobacco, rice and later cotton, which had been produced by slave labour.

The triangle, involving three continents, was complete. European capital, African labour and American land and resources combined to supply a European market.

By the 1730s about 15 ships a year were leaving for Africa and this grew to about 50 a year in the 1750s, rising to just over a 100 in each of the early years of the 1770s. Numbers declined during the American War of Independence (1775-1783), but rose to a new peak of 120-130 ships annually in the two decades preceding the abolition of the slave trade in 1807. Probably three-quarters of all European slaving ships at this period left from Liverpool. Overall, Liverpool ships transported half of the three million Africans carried across the Atlantic by British slavers.

Conditions On Board

Conditions on board ship from Africa to the New World were appalling. The combination of over-crowding, disease, inadequate food, poor weather, unseaworthy ships, rebellion and punishment took a heavy toll on captives and crew alike. Surviving records suggest that until the 1750s one in five Africans on board ship died.

Male slaves were packed together below deck and were secured by leg irons. The space was so cramped they were forced to crouch or lie down. Women and children were kept in separate quarters, sometimes on deck, allowing them limited freedom of movement, but this also exposed them to violence and sexual abuse from the crew.

Some European governments, such as the British and French, introduced laws to control conditions on board. They reduced the numbers of slaves to be carried and required a surgeon to be taken on each voyage. The principal reason for taking action was concern for the crew and not the captives. The surgeons, though often unqualified, were paid head-money to keep slaves alive. By about 1800 records show that the number of Africans who died had declined to about one in 18.

Liverpool's Fortune

A significant factor in Liverpool's engagement in the Slave Trade was the port's geographical position in the north-west of England, with ready access via a network of rivers and canals to the goods traded in Africa - textiles from Lancashire and Yorkshire, copper and brass from Staffordshire and Cheshire and guns from Birmingham.

Liverpool's first slaving vessel, ironically named Blessing, set sail in 1700. In 1710 two slave ships departed from Liverpool, 24 from London and 20 from Bristol. London then declined and Bristol rose to prominence mid-century, but by 1771 Liverpool was the pre-eminent slave ship port. That year no fewer than 107 left dock on the Mersey on slaving voyages compared with 58 from London and 20 from Bristol. By the end of the 18th century, Liverpool had over 60% of the entire British trade and 40% of the entire European slave trade.

Profits could be huge: the ship Lively made a profit of 300% in 1737, although this was exceptional. Most ships could guarantee a 10% profit.

In Liverpool, there were ten large merchant houses engaged in the slave trade and 349 smaller firms. Shop windows displayed shining chains and manacles, devices to force open the mouths of slaves who refused to eat, neck rings, thumb screws and other implements of torment and oppression.

Not all of Liverpool's wealth was thanks to the slave trade, but it was undoubtedly the backbone of the town's prosperity. Slaving and related trades may have occupied a third and possibly a half of Liverpool's shipping activity in the period 1750 to 1807. The wealth acquired by the town was substantial and the stimulus it gave to trading and industrial development throughout the north-west of England and the Midlands was of crucial importance.

Slave merchants such as Foster Cunliffe made a fortune. He was mayor of the city three times and President of the Liverpool Infirmary and a sponsor of the Bluecoat School. When he wasn't exercising his philanthropic impulses, he sent three or four ships to collect African slaves each year in the 1730s. Before his death, Foster Cunliffe had ensured his son Ellis a seat in parliament. Other families such as the Leylands, Bolds and Kennions prospered in a similar way.

Defending the slave trade in the British Parliament in 1806, Liverpool's MP, General Bonastre Tarleton, himself from a slave-owning family, described with pride Liverpool's rise 'to become the second place in wealth and population in the British Empire'. During the same debate,

William Roscoe and William Wilberforce worked on behalf of the Society for the Abolition of the Slave Trade and were adamant that 'nothing short of an entire and immediate abolition will satisfy'. The Parliamentary vote resulted in the abolition of slavery in Britain the following year.

The last British slaver, the Kitty's Amelia, under Captain Hugh Crow, a one-eyed Manxman, left Liverpool in July, 1807.

Source: http://h2g2.com/edited_entry/A2408889

By the 18th century, slavery was seen as essential to Britain's economy and power, and therefore accepted as the norm. The profits had given merchants and planters involved enough wealth and power to found banks and other financial institutions, and acquire immense political power. Between 1787 and 1807 all the Mayors of Liverpool were involved in the slave trade and 50 or 60 MPs represented slave plantations. They were able to build stately homes, marry into the aristocracy, and invest in industrial enterprises. William Beckford, twice Lord Mayor of London and owner of a 22,000 acre estate in Jamaica, left his son one million pounds and £100,000 a year in his will.

Web Source: http://www.recoveredhistories.org/storiesproslavery.php

----

After The Slave Trade

Vestiges that Remain

After abolition in Britain in 1807 Liverpool continued to develop the trading connections which had been established by the slave trade, both in Africa and the Americas. It continued to grow and prosper as a maritime port well into the 20th Century, until sea trade declined internationally and the demand for new ships from the Mersey shipyards reduced to such a level that they are now closed.

The Maritime Museum with its gallery detailing the city's role in the trade stands on the corner of Albert Dock. Built in 1841, the dock is next to the former entrance of Canning Dock, Liverpool's first dock used by the slave ships and today filled in and known as Canning Place. Two dry docks used to repair slave ships from the 1750s until the end of the trade are still used today by the Maritime Museum. Aside from this, some buildings of the era survive scattered around the town.

The Bluecoats School, founded and funded by slave merchants, is now an arts centre.

At Pier Head, buildings resonant of the British Empire such as the Liver Building dominate a landscape whose wealth was built with the slave ships that once docked just a few hundred yards away.

The city of Liverpool now officially acknowledges the fact of it once being a major slaving port with the opening of the International Slavery Museum on 23 August, 2007.

Liverpool: Britain's Main Slaving Port

Fact: Liverpool merchants developed expert knowledge of the trade and established good contacts with traders on the African coast. They knew which goods to send to Africa and very importantly which goods would sell on different parts of the coast.

During the 18th century Liverpool was Britain's main slaving port. Between 1700 and 1807, ships from Liverpool carried about 1.5 million Africans across the Atlantic in conditions of great cruelty. Most Liverpool ships went to the islands of the Caribbean where captains sold the Africans to plantations owners. The owners and their agents forced the Africans to work as chattel slaves producing sugar and other tropical goods. They treated the enslaved brutally and showed little concern for their personal lives. The trade generally operated on a triangular basis. Merchants fitted out and supplied their ships in Liverpool. The ships carried goods to West Africa including textiles, firearms, alcohol, beads and cowries shells. On arrival at the coast, captains bartered and sold these goods for Africans. The voyage across the Atlantic usually took six to eight weeks, but sometimes longer. Conditions on board were appalling and many Africans died. Many Africans resisted enslavement and revolts on the ships were a regular occurrence. When the captains had sold their captives, the ships returned to Liverpool, generally with goods such as sugar, coffee, cocoa, cotton, tobacco and wood.

The first known slave ship to sail from Liverpool was the Liverpool Merchant, which left the port on 3 October 1699 and carried 220 Africans to Barbados. The trade grew slowly over the next 20 years but then developed rapidly. By 1750 Liverpool had overtaken Bristol and London, and the town's ships dominated the trade until abolition in 1807. In the 1790s Liverpool controlled 80% of the British slave trade and over 40% of the European slave trade. The reasons for Liverpool's control of the trade are varied. Her geographical position meant that merchants had easy access to the goods that would sell in Africa. These included textiles from Lancashire and Yorkshire, pottery, copper and brass from Staffordshire and Cheshire and guns from Birmingham. Merchants also strengthened trading links to London, Amsterdam and other European ports to obtain luxury silks and other textiles from India, glass beads from Italy and cowries from the Indian Ocean. But crucially, Liverpool merchants developed expert knowledge of the trade and established good contacts with traders on the African coast. They knew which goods to send to Africa and very importantly which goods would sell on different parts of the coast.

Much of Liverpool's wealth came from slavery. From about 1750 until 1807, between a third and a half of Liverpool's trade was with Africa and the Caribbean. Virtually all the leading inhabitants of the town, including the Mayors, Town Councillors and MPs, invested in the slave trade and profited from it. The prosperity and growth of the town was closely connected with its involvement with slavery. When the campaign to abolish the trade began in the 1780s, opposition in the town was strong. Several Liverpudlians spoke in favour of the trade at the parliamentary inquiries and the most prominent were given valuable gifts from the Town Council and several were given the freedom of the borough. A few local abolitionists, like William Roscoe, worked behind the scenes but generally chose not to engage in public debate.

After the abolition of the slave trade in 1807, merchants in the town used their contacts to maintain trading with Africa and the Americas. Several former slave merchants and captains developed a very profitable trade in African palm oil and by degrees Liverpool came to dominate all British trade with West Africa. This control was maintained until after the Second World War. Whilst sugar and the other tropical goods continued to be imported from the Caribbean, the biggest growth was in imported raw cotton from the southern states of America. This was produced by slave labour on plantations until 1865. Cotton was a major factor in Liverpool's growth in the 19th century and helps to explain why support for the Confederate cause during the American Civil War was so strong. The economic benefits also extended to Manchester, other towns in Lancashire and the wider British economy.

Although the vast majority of Africans transported by Liverpool ships were taken to the Americas, there were a few Black people in Liverpool in the 18th century. Most would have been domestic servants and whilst not treated as harshly as the chattel slaves on the plantations, their lives would have been strictly controlled. There are several documented sales of Blacks in Liverpool - the largest a sale of 11 Africans at the Exchange Coffee House in 1766. A few local Black people today can trace their family back to the late 18th century and many others are descended from Africans who came to Liverpool as a result of the trade between West Africa and Liverpool in the 19th century.

Web Source: www.liverpoolmuseums.org.uk/maritime/archive/info-sheet.aspx?

Vestiges that Remain

There is still evidence of Liverpool's role in the slave trade around the city centre. Bold, Tarleton and Cunliffe Streets in the city centre are amongst many streets named after merchants who were involved in the trade. Many buildings, including the Town Hall, were built with wealth created by the trade. In 1994 a permanent gallery, Transatlantic Slavery: Against Human Dignity, was opened in the Merseyside Maritime Museum. This has been replaced with the new International Slavery Museum (opened 23rd August 2007).

Seagoing Vessels Trading from Liverpool to the Coast of Africa (Slave Trade)

Dominant involvement of Liverpool (5300 voyages), London (3100 voyages) and Bristol (2200 voyages) which between them accounted for over 90% of the British trade. And the process of domination seems to have accelerated at the end of the century with Liverpool not only outstripping its English rivals but the European competition. In the two decades preceding abolition, Liverpool was responsible for 75% of all slaving voyages across Europe.

There is no doubt that slaving became a specialist trade. A slave voyage was quite complex to organise and the balance of trade goods was crucial. Knowledge and experience were the keys to success. Merchants gave their captains detailed letters of instruction with very specific instructions. The range and relatively quantities of goods was also vitally important. The relationship between merchants in Europe and African traders was quite sophisticated and personal contacts developed and helped sustain it. Often ships carried quite small parcels of goods and sometimes there were specific requests. The investment was also high - by the late eighteenth century it was costing £10-12,000 to outfit a vessel, a very significant sum. The return on that investment was also relatively slow not only because of the length of the voyages, but it frequently took 3-6 months to obtain a cargo of enslaved Africans on the west African coast. This is partly why many vessels chose to return to Europe without waiting for a cargo in the Caribbean and came back with bills of exchange, which were negotiable.

A List of Vessels trading from Liverpool to the Coast of Africa, with their Commanders and Owners Names , what Part of the Coast each Ship goes to, and for what number of Slaves. December, 1752.

Africa, -- Hallison, Benin, John Welsh and Company	250
Antigua Merchant, Robert Thomas , Angola, James Gildart and Co	206
Annabella, Wm Harrison, Wind. and Gold Coast, W. Dobb & Co	260
Anglesea, J Caruthers, Wind. and Gold Coast, T Farrer and Co	180
Alice Galley, R. Jackson, Wind. and Gold Coast, Robert Cheshyre and Co	350
Ann Galley, Neh Holland, Callabar, William Whalley and Co	340
Adlington, T. Perkin, Windward and Gold Coast, J. Manesty & Co	320

African, John Newton, Windward and Gold Coast, J. Manesty and Co 250

Allen, James Strangeways, Windward and Gold Coast, John Brooks and Co 250

Achilles, Thomas Patrick, --, Henry Hardwar and Co 450

Barbadoes Merchant, John Wilson, Angola, G. Campbell and Co 500

Betty, Samuel Sacheveril, John Robinson 200

Blake, Alexander Torbett, Callabar, John Bird and Co 460

Boyne, William Wilkinson, Bonny, Edward Forbes and Co 400

Beverley, William Lowe, Angola, Edward Lowndes and Co 200

Brooke, Thomas Kewley, Old Callabar, Roger Brooks and Co 400

Barclay, John Gadson, Old Callabar, John Welsh and Co 450

Bulkeley, C. Baitson, Wind. and Gold Coast, F Cunliffe Sons & Co 350

Britannia, James Pemberton, Wind. and Gold Coast, Leatherbarrow and Co 300

Bridget, --- Hayston, Wind. and Gold Coast, F Cunliffe Sons and Co 250

Chesterfield, Patrick Black, Old Calabar, William Whalley and Co 440

Clayton, (taken by Pirates & retaken by a Por. M.W.),--, J. Clayton & Co 440

Cumberland, John Griffin, Gambia, Ed. Deane and Co 260

Charming Nancy, T Roberts, W and Gold Coast, W Davenport and Co 170

Cavendish, R Jennings, W and Gold Coast, Rd Nicholas and Co 170

Cecilia, Rd. Younge, Gambia, Fr. Green and Co 120

Duke of Cumberland, John Crosbie , Bonny, James Crosbie and Co 450

Dolphin, Joseph Pederick, Wind. and Gold Coast, Ed. Forbes and Co 200

Enterprize, Samuel Greenhow, Gambia, (missing) John Yates and Co 130

Elijah, ---, Windward and Gold Coast, Edward Lowndes and Co 200

Elizabeth, William Heys, Gambia, Samuel Shaw and Co	200
Ellis & Robert, R Jackson, W and G. Coast, F. Cunliffe Sons & Co	320
Eaton, John Hughes, Angola, J. Okill and Co. (wood and teeth)	550
Fanny, Wm Jenkinson, Wind. and Gold Coast, J. Knight and Co	120
Florimell, Samuel Linecar, Callabar, Richard Townsend and Co	320
Frodsham, James Powell, Angola, Nish. Torr and Co	450
Fortune, Hugh Williams, Bonny, Henry Townsend and Co	450
Foster, Edward Cropper, Benin, Foster Cunliffe Sons and Co	200
Ferret, Joseph Welch, Windward Coast &c., John Welch and Co	50
George, Charles Cooke, Angola, G. Campbell and Co	250
Grace,--, Old Callabar, Edward Forbes and Co	400
Greyhound,--, Windward and Gold Coast, R. Savage and Co	120
Hesketh, James Thompson, New Callabar, R. Nicholas and Co	260
Hector, Brook Keelsall, New Callabar, William Gregson and Co	480
Hardman, Joseph Yoward, W. and G. Coast, John Hardman and Co	300
Jenny, Thomas Derbyshire, W. & G. Coast, J. Knight and Co	450
Judith, N. Southworth, Bonny, John Welch and Co	350
James, John Sacheverill, Wind. and Gold Coast, James Gildart	120
Knight, Wm. Boates, Wind. and Gold Coast, John Knight and Co	400
Lintott, Ralph Lowe, New Callabar, Richard Nicholas and Co	400
Lord Strange, Edward Smith, Benin, Wm. Halliday and Co	230
Lovely Betty, G. Jackson, W. and G. Coast, G. Campbell and Co	140
Little Billy, T. Dickinson, W. and G. Coast, John Knight and Co	60

Mersey, John Gee, Benin, John Kennion and Co	300
Middleham, John Welch, Old Callabar, Richard Gildart and Sons	320
Methwen, John Coppell, Wind. and G. Coast, James Crosbie and Co	280
Minerva, Thomas Jordan, Gambia, James Pardoe and Co	400
Mercury, John Walker, W. and G. Coast, Konnien and Holme	100
Molly, Richard Rigby, W. and G. Coast, Richard Golding and Co	320
Neptune, T. Thompson, Old Calibar, Joseph and Jona. Brooks & Co	450
Nelly, John Simmons, Old Calibar, William Williamson and Co	340
Nancy , John Honeyford, Bonny, Thomas Kendal and Co	400
Nancy, Robert Hewitt, Bonny, Peter Holme and Co	400
Nancy, Thomas Midglev, Gambia, Knight Mairs and Co	300
Orrell, James Griffin, Gambia, William Whaley and Co	120
Ormond Success,--, Angola, William Williamson and Co	300
Pardoe,--,Windward and Gold Coast, James Pardoe and Co	240
Priscilla, William Parkinson, Angola, John Welch and Co	350
Phoebe, W. Lawson, W. and G. Coast, A. and B. Heywood and Co	280
Prince William, John Valentine, Angola, P. Gildart aad Sons	200
Rider, Michael Ruth, Angola, Richard Gildart and Sons	300
Ranger, J. Sander's, Wind. and Gold Coast, W. Farrington and Co	300
Sterling Castle, Charles Gardner, Bonny, John Backhouse and Co	300
Sarah, A. Lawson, Bonny, Thomas Crowder and Co	550
Salisbury, T. Marsden, Old Callabar, Robert Armitage and Co	350
Samuel and Nancy, J. Lowe, W. and Gold Coast, R. Savage and Co	220

Swan, Peter Leay, Bonny, John Tarleton and Co	400
Sammy and Biddy, R. Grayson, Wind Coast &c., J. Blundell & Co	150
Schemer, Robert Grimshaw, Wind Coast &c., T. Chalmers and Co	120
Stronge, T Cubbin, Bonny, M. and J Stronge and Co	300
Tarlton, J. Thompson, Bonny, John Tarlton and Co	340
Triton, Charles Jenkinson, Bonny, Levinus Unsworth and Co	240
Thomas, J. Hutchinson, Gambia, George Campbell and Co	200
True Blue, Ben Wade, Benin, John Cheshyre and Co	300
Thomas and Martha, J. Gillman, W. & G Coast, G Campbell & Co	200
Vigilant, W. Freeman, W. & G Coast, (missing) J. Bridge and Co	160
Union, T. Anyon, W. & G Coast, James Pardoe and Co	350
William and Betty, Thomas Barclay, Angola, Samuel Shawe and Co	400

Sources:

http://boards.ancestry.com/topics.ethnic.afam.slaveinfo/465/mb.ashx?pnt=1

http://www.liverpoolmuseums.org.uk/ism/resources/slave_trade_ports.aspx

The 1805 Directory of Liverpool, by Gore. pp 112 thru 115

The Triangular Trade: Liverpool and Slavery

The 'Triangular Trade' was another name for the Slave Trade, and it was so called because this consisted of trade goods (such as pottery and earthenware, cheap jewellery, items of clothing and linen, and small knives and axes – mostly manufactured in towns like Manchester and Sheffield) being shipped from Britain to Africa. These were then exchanged, with African Slavers, for men, women, and children whom they had abducted from their homes.

The captives were then transported, shackled together in the holds of the same ships, to the sugar cane, cotton, and tobacco plantations of America and the West Indies. Produce from these was then carried back to Liverpool, to be processed, sold, and transported onwards to the rest of Britain and its expanding Empire.

Because the Slave Trade generated so much income for the Town, and its merchants, Liverpool actively encouraged and invested heavily in this traffic in human life and misery. Few people, at least in the early days of the Trade, felt any guilt about what they were doing; Slavery had been a normal and socially acceptable business throughout Britain since 1562, when the first regular trading took place with Africa.

The first recorded slaving ship to set sail from Liverpool was 'The Liverpool Merchant', which sold a cargo of 220 slaves in Barbados, in 1700. Then, in 1737, Liverpool began to invest seriously in the Triangular Trade. Vast fortunes were made for many Liverpool ship owners and, in 1771 alone, 105 ships sailed from Liverpool to West Africa, and from there transported 28,200 slaves to the West Indies.

Small numbers of slaves, of both sexes and all ages, were brought to Liverpool and were occasionally sold at local auctions. Others became house slaves for the more wealthy families in the Town: Black domestic servants in great houses were seen as a conspicuous sign of wealth at that time and, whilst some were paid wages and could leave their employers, others were treated as property or as 'fashion statements'.

In Liverpool's International Slavery Museum at the Albert Dock, the galleries and exhibits are a moving and disturbing exposure of the City's association with Slavery. The vivid portrayals of the violent seizure from their villages, of peaceful and settled people, and of their subsequent transportation in the bowels of squalid ships, are powerful indeed. Most heart-rending though, are the descriptions of the reality of transportation across the Atlantic, on the notorious 'Middle Passage' of a vessel's triangular route, and which could take 50-60 days, often in appalling weather conditions.

Packed tightly together naked, on hard, wooden shelves - the sexes and ages often randomly mixed, these people were manacled and chained with no room to move. Fed only on subsistence levels of gruel or thin soup, with no way to relieve themselves other than where they lay, and, afflicted by sea-sickness, dysentery, and terror, the conditions were foul beyond belief.

Many thousands of people did not survive the journey, and the personal testimonies of those that did, and of their descendants, serve to clearly illustrate just how Liverpool became wealthy, and Britain became 'Great', through this exploitation of humanity. Indeed, a fifth of all slaves died during the Atlantic crossing, and only 60% of those who did make land survived for more than a year in captivity. Of those, most only lived into their 30s.

It is estimated that, from the middle of the 15th Century to the end of the 19th Century, more than 12 million Africans were kidnapped from their homes. In the 18th Century alone, 6 million African slaves were transported to the American plantations and, shamefully, Britain had the largest slave trading fleets.

Liverpool was Britain's most 'successful' slave-trading port, and during the City's involvement in the trade 1,360,000 African people were transported in over 5,000 voyages made by Liverpool vessels. Indeed, more than half of all slaves sold by English traders were the property of Liverpool merchants and, by the end of the 18th Century, the Town had 70% of Britain's Slave Trade.

But then, the attitude to Slavery began to change in Britain and, in 1787, a petition for the suppression of the Slave Trade was handed to Parliament by some members of the Society of Friends (Quakers). Because of this action, in 1788, Liverpool Town Corporation formally declared its opposition to the abolition of the Slave Trade, although it is important to note that there was a large, vocal, and well-organised abolitionist movement in Liverpool, led by powerful merchants and philanthropists – such as William Roscoe, who were supported, significantly, by large numbers of influential and prominent women in the Town.

Eventually, and following years of public meetings and acrimonious debate, and despite protectionism and downright ignorance by vested interests, in 1807, an 'Act for the Abolition of The Transatlantic Slave Trade' was carried through Parliament. This outlawed the transportation of slaves by British ships, thus beginning the end of the Triangular Trade.

However, the subsequent 'Slavery Abolition Act' was not passed until 1830; only coming into force in 1834. This freed all slaves in the Caribbean, although those in some other British colonies had to wait longer for their own emancipation. In fact, freed slaves in the West Indies were forced to undertake a period of 'apprenticeship' - working for former masters for a pittance - which meant that Slavery across the British Empire was not in fact completely abolished until 1838.

It is also important to note that, whilst former slave-ship, slave, and plantation owners received massive financial compensation for their losses, former slaves received nothing for theirs.

Despite this loss of a highly lucrative source of revenue, the Port of Liverpool and its maritime trade continued to thrive, thanks to families such as the Rathbones, Holts, Rankins, and Bibbys. These were a new breed of entrepreneurial ship-owners, trading in a variety of goods other than in human bondage. Such prominent individuals laid the foundation for Liverpool's massive expansion, and its more wholesome economic success, during the 19th and early 20th centuries. Indeed, Liverpool's peak of economic success was achieved in the half-Century following abolition, and its highest population – 867,000 – was achieved in 1937.

Nevertheless, it should be remembered too, that Slavery in many forms still exists today, in many countries of the world.

Web Source: http://www.discover-liverpool.com/24/section.aspx/7

Liverpool's Acknowledged Legacy of Slave Trade

Liverpool's most successful merchants tended to live more modestly within the town itself than their French counterparts. However, they also invested in houses on the outskirts of the town or sometimes further afield. Thomas Leyland had several unexceptional houses in Liverpool during his lifetime but also acquired Walton Hall north of the city (in fact not a stunning architectural building!). The Ashtons bought Woolton Hall, which was in a different league, especially after it was remodelled by Robert Adam, the leading architect and interior decorator of the age.

But the influences of slavery could be more specific. Liverpool's Town Hall is known for its frieze including African heads, elephants and crocodiles - but similar African masks are found on buildings in Nantes and in Bordeaux. Street names reflect not only the names of slave traders - again in Liverpool, Earle, Tarleton, Cunliffe but also in names like Goree (the slave island off Dakar) and Jamaica Street, and in Bristol again Jamaica Street, Guinea Street and Black Boy Hill.

Many of the ports have stories about the slave trade passed on by word of mouth and in popular histories. Liverpudlians are very familiar with the stories of tunnels under the city for transporting slaves between the docks and the town and the cellars where they are said to have been kept and shackled. But one can find similar tales of tunnels and cellars in Bristol and in Nantes. Perhaps more surprisingly, there are stories of slaves being kept in the cellars of isolated farmhouses in Morecambe Bay and working in the local quarries - a reflection of Lancaster's brief foray into the trade.

The wealth deriving from the slave trade was reflected not only in the buildings and general economic climate but in the fortunes of the individual participants. In Liverpool, we know that every major merchant and thus every major citizen, was involved to a greater or less extent in the slave trade and its benefits. It is often quoted that all the Mayors of the town from the mid-eighteenth century until 1807 (and it includes the other civic officials) had slaving links. But some were more involved that others. William Davenport was involved in 140 voyages. John Tarleton, mayor in 1764, saw his fortune increase from £6000 in 1748 to £80,000 by 1773. Thomas Leyland, three times Mayor, left nearly £750,000 in 1827 and was involved in a range of activities, including founding a bank.

Acknowledgement of past involvement in the slave trade

But there are other sorts of legacies, apart from the economic ones. One important one is how the ports and their inhabitants have dealt with their past involvement with slaving. There is no doubt that on a popular level, knowledge of the slaving past has been an important part of the inhabitants' consciousness for a long time. In large part this has probably been sustained by the stories of tunnels, of secret cellars and slaves being sold or chained up - regularly repeated in the local press over the last century and supported in popular literature. In Liverpool, as early as 1884, "A Dickey Sam" published Liverpool and Slavery: A History of the Liverpool-African Slave Trade and this was followed by more comprehensive works such as Gomer Williams' 1897 history of the Liverpool privateering and slaving.

However, at an official level, the slave trade was generally perceived as something best forgotten. This is reflected in the treatment of the long-standing Black populations, certainly in the British and French ports, which have been marginalised, neglected and disadvantaged. The situation has changed in the last 20 to 30 years and the importance of the slave trade in the history of the slave ports has been increasingly on the agenda. Partly this is as a result of the work of academics. But it is also as a result of lobbying by the Black populations themselves, looking primarily for recognition and acknowledgement of the past, and by a realisation amongst some whites that this is an important issue.

In Nantes, two major international academic conferences have been held, the first in 1975. The city also has two organisations memorialising the involvement and lobbying for greater recognition. One of them, Les Anneaux de la Mèmoires, was closely involved in the temporary exhibition which was held in the museum in 1992. The civic authorities supported the exhibition, but the process of achieving it was by no means an easy or simple project.

Liverpool had its first conference on the trade in 1976, though it dealt with the British trade and lacked the international involvement that was a key feature of the one in Nantes. The opening of the Transatlantic Slavery Gallery in the Maritime Museum in October 1994 saw the first permanent gallery devoted to the subject in any of the slave ports. The gallery has had a significant impact both in the city and wider afield. Bristol has been slower to come to terms with its involvement and more reluctant. The City Museum in Bristol held a major temporary exhibition on Bristol and the slave trade in 1999, the core of which has now been installed in the Industrial Museum. On a wider basis, the National Maritime Museum at Greenwich has incorporated a section on the slave trade in its Trade and Empire Gallery also opened in 1999. The Commonwealth and Empire Museum to be based in Bristol plans to include significant reference to the subject. The National Maritime Museum in Amsterdam, another slaving port, is considering a temporary exhibition of the Dutch trade and determining how the subject can be permanently incorporated in the major refurbishment of their museum.

There is thus some recognition in the former slave ports that the slaving past needs to be recognised. There is obviously a long way to go and more that can be done. And there are also some wider movements beginning to unfold. In 1993 UNESCO began its Slave Route project, an attempt to recognise the importance and consequences of the slave trade on an international basis and in particularly to seek the assistance of Europeans in helping both African, Caribbean and South American nations in this process. In this sense, the triangle which began as a trading arrangement is being re-established to memorialise it. The slave trade completely changed the history of three continents; but it also profoundly changed the ports that organised it and they are still struggling to live with the consequences

Web Source: http://www.liverpoolmuseums.org.uk/ism/resources/slave_trade_ports.aspx

The following are two chapters relating to Liverpool and the Slave Trade from:

THE HISTORY OF THE RISE, PROGRESS, AND ACCOMPLISHMENT OF THE ABOLITION OF THE SLAVE-TRADE, BY THE BRITISH PARLIAMENT

By

THOMAS CLARKSON, M.A.   1839

CHAPTER XVII.

Author secures the Gloucester paper, and lays the foundation of a petition from that city; does the same at Worcester, and at Chester.—Arrives at Liverpool.—Collects specimens of African produce; also imports and exports, and muster-rolls, and accounts of dock duties, and iron instruments used in the Slave Trade.—His introduction to Mr. Norris, and others.—Author and his errand become known.—People visit him out of curiosity.—Frequent controversies on the subject of the Slave Trade.

On my arrival at Gloucester, I waited upon my friend Dean Tucker. He was pleased to hear of the great progress I had made since he left me. On communicating to him my intention of making interest with the editors of some provincial papers, to enlighten the public mind, and with the inhabitants of some respectable places, for petitions to Parliament, relative to the abolition of the Slave Trade, he approved of it, and introduced me to Mr. Raikes, the proprietor of the respectable paper belonging to that city. Mr. Raikes acknowledged, without any hesitation, the pleasure he should have in serving such a noble cause; and he promised to grant me, from time to time, a corner in his paper, for such things as I might point out to him for insertion. This promise he performed afterwards, without any pecuniary consideration, and solely on the ground of benevolence. He promised also his assistance as to the other object, for the promotion of which I left him several of my *Summary View* to distribute.

At Worcester I trod over the same ground, and with the same success. Timothy Bevington, of the religious society of the Quakers, was the only person to whom I had an introduction there: he accompanied me to the mayor, to the editor of the Worcester paper, and to several others, before each of whom I pleaded the cause of the oppressed Africans in the best manner I was able. I dilated both on the inhumanity and on the impolicy of the trade, which I supported by the various facts recently obtained at Bristol. I desired, however, as far as petitions were concerned, (and this desire I expressed on all other similar occasions,) that no attempt should be made to obtain these, till such information had been circulated on the subject, that every one, when called upon, might judge, from his knowledge of it, how far he would feel it right to join in it. For this purpose I left also here several of my *Summary View* for distribution.

After my arrival at Chester, I went to the bishop's residence, but I found he was not there. Knowing no other person in the place, I wrote a note to Mr. Cowdroy, whom I understood to be the editor of the Chester paper, soliciting an interview with him, I explained my wishes to him on both subjects. He seemed to be greatly rejoiced, when we met, that such a measure as that of the abolition of the Slave Trade was in contemplation. Living at so short a distance from Liverpool, and in a country from which so many persons were constantly going to Africa, he was by no means ignorant, as some were, of the nature of this cruel traffic; but yet he had no notion that I had probed it so deeply, or that I had brought to light such important circumstances concerning it, as he found by my conversation. He made me a hearty offer of his services on this occasion, and this expressly without fee or reward. I accepted them most joyfully and gratefully. It was, indeed, a most important thing, to have a station so near the enemy's camp, where we could watch their motions, and meet any attack which might be made from it. And this office of a sentinel Mr. Cowdroy performed with great vigilance; and when he afterwards left Chester for Manchester, to establish a paper there, he carried with him the same friendly disposition towards our cause.

My first introduction at Liverpool was to William Rathbone, a member of the religious society of the Quakers. He was the same person who, before the formation of our committee, had procured me copies of several of the muster-rolls of the slave-vessels belonging to that port, so that, though we were not personally known, yet we were not strangers to each other. Isaac Hadwen, a respectable member of the same society, was the person whom I saw next. I had been introduced to him, previously to my journey, when he was at London, at the yearly meeting of the Quakers, so that no letter to him was necessary. As Mr. Roscoe had generally given the profits of *The Wrongs of Africa* to our committee, I made no scruple of calling upon him. His reception of me was very friendly, and he introduced me afterwards to Dr. Currie, who had written the preface to that poem. There was also a fourth upon whom I called, though I did not know him. His name was Edward Rushton: he had been an officer in a slave-ship, but had lost his sight, and had become an enemy to that trade. On passing through Chester, I had heard, for the first time, that he had published a poem called *West Indian Eclogues*, with a view of making the public better acquainted with the evil of the Slave Trade, and of exciting their indignation against it. Of the three last it may be observed, that, having come forward thus early, as labourers, they deserve to be put down, as I have placed them in the map, among the forerunners and coadjutors in this great cause, for each published his work before any efforts were made publicly, or without knowing that any were intended. Rushton, also, had the boldness, though then living in Liverpool, to affix his name to his work. These were the only persons whom I knew for some time after my arrival in that place.

It may not, perhaps, be necessary to enter so largely into my proceedings at Liverpool as at Bristol. The following account, therefore, may suffice:—

In my attempts to add to my collection of specimens of African produce, I was favoured with a sample of gum ruber astringents, of cotton from the Gambia, of indigo and musk, of long pepper, of black pepper from Whidàh, of mahogany from Calabar, and of cloths of different colours, made by the natives, which, while they gave other proofs of the quality of their own cotton, gave proofs, also, of the variety of their dyes.

I made interest at the Custom-house for various exports and imports, and for copies of the muster-rolls of several slave-vessels, besides those of vessels employed in other trades.

By looking out constantly for information on this great subject, I was led to the examination of a printed card or table of the dock duties of Liverpool, which was published annually. The town of Liverpool had so risen in opulence and importance from only a fishing-village, that the corporation seemed to have a pride in giving a public view of this increase. Hence they published and circulated this card. Now the card contained one, among other facts, which was almost as precious, in a political point of view, as any I had yet obtained. It stated that in the year 1772, when I knew that a hundred vessels sailed out of Liverpool for the coast of Africa, the dock-duties amounted to 4552*l.*, and that in 1779, when I knew that, in consequence of the war, only eleven went from thence to the same coast, they amounted to 4957*l.* From these facts put together, two conclusions were obvious. The first was, that the opulence of Liverpool, as far as the entry of vessels into its ports, and the dock-duties arising from thence, were concerned, was not indebted to the Slave Trade; for these duties were highest when it had only eleven ships in that employ. The second was, that there had been almost a practical experiment with respect to the abolition of it; for the vessels in it had been gradually reduced from one hundred to eleven, and yet the West Indians had not complained of their ruin, nor had the merchants or manufacturers suffered, nor had Liverpool been affected by the change.

There were specimens of articles in Liverpool, which I entirely overlooked at Bristol, and which I believed I should have overlooked here also, had it not been for seeing them at a window in a shop; I mean those of different iron instruments used in this cruel traffic. I bought a pair of the iron hand-cuffs with which the men-slaves are confined. The right-hand wrist of one, and the left of another, are almost brought into contact by these, and fastened together, as the figure A in the annexed plate represents, by a little bolt with a small padlock at the end of it.

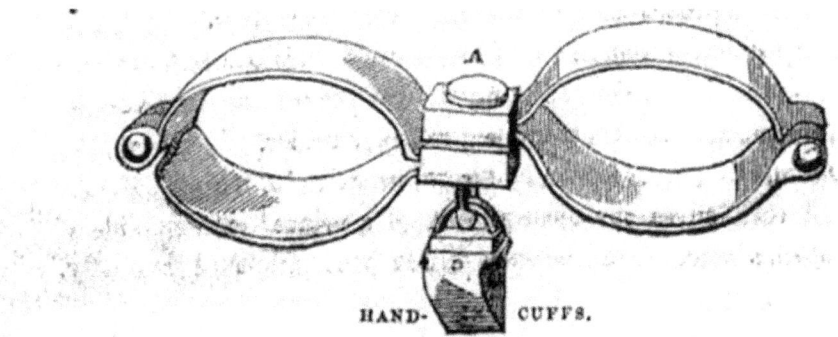

HAND-	CUFFS.

I bought also a pair of shackles for the legs. These are represented by the figure B.

The right ancle of one man is fastened to the left of another, as the reader will observe, by similar means. I bought these, not because it was difficult to conceive how the unhappy victims of this execrable trade were confined, but to show the fact that they were so. For what was the inference from it, but that they did not leave their own country willingly; that, when they were in the holds of the slave-vessels, they were not in the Elysium which had been represented; and that there was a fear either that they would make their escape, or punish their oppressors?

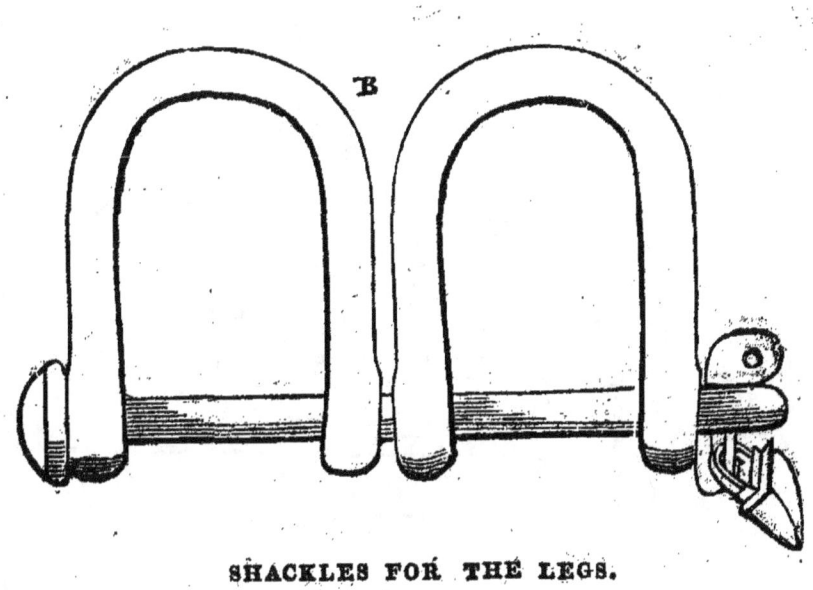

SHACKLES FOR THE LEGS.

Figure 6. Shackles for the Legs

I bought also a thumb-screw at this shop. The thumbs are put into this instrument through the two circular holes at the top of it. By turning a key, a bar rises up by means of a screw from C to D, and the pressure upon them becomes painful. By turning it further you may make the blood start from the ends of them. By taking the key away, as at E, you leave the tortured person in agony, without any means of extricating himself, or of being extricated by others. This screw, as I was then informed, was applied by way of punishment, in case of obstinacy in the slaves, or for any other reputed offence, at the discretion of the captain.

At the same place I bought another instrument which I saw. It was called a speculum oris. The dotted lines in the figure on the right hand of the screw represent it when shut, the black lines when open. It is opened, as at G H, by a screw below with a nob at the end of it. This instrument is known among surgeons, having been invented to assist them in wrenching open the mouth as in the case of a locked jaw; but it had got into use in this trade.

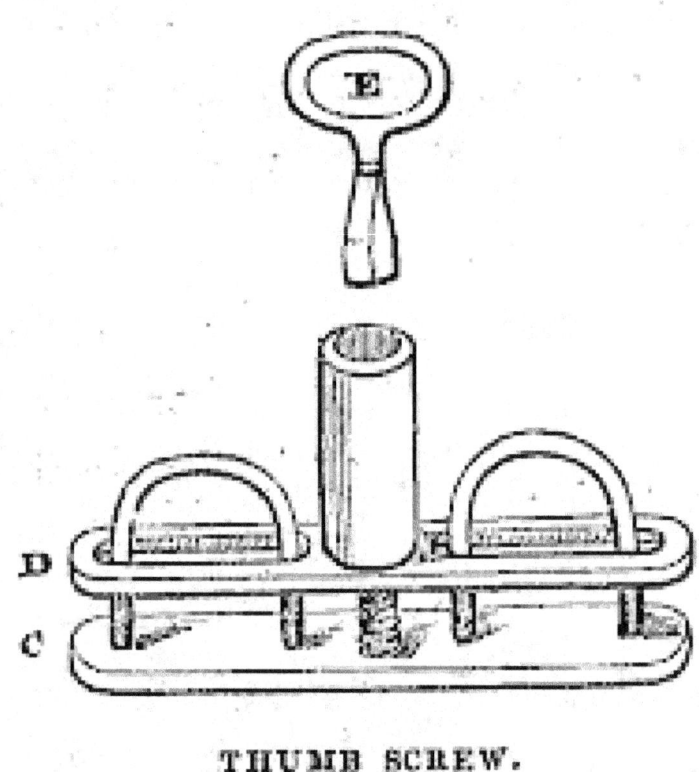

THUMB SCREW.

Figure 7. Thumb Screw

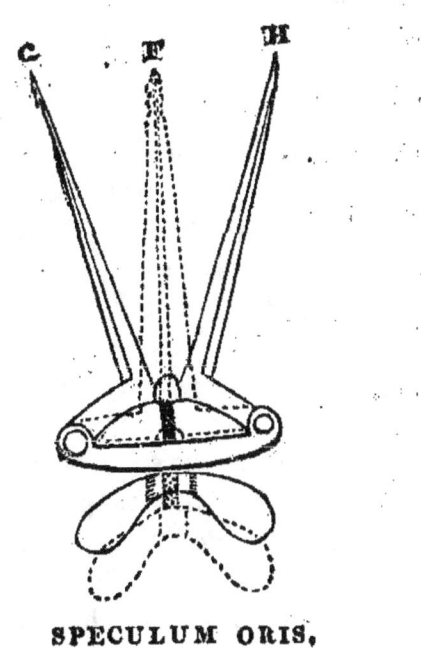

SPECULUM ORIS,

Figure 8. Speculum Oris

On asking the seller of the instruments on what occasion it was used there, he replied that the slaves were frequently so sulky as to shut their mouths against all sustenance, and this with a determination to die; and that it was necessary their mouths should be forced open to throw in nutriment, that they who had purchased them might incur no loss by their death.

The town-talk of Liverpool was much of the same nature as that at Bristol on the subject of this trade. Horrible facts concerning it were in everybody's mouth; but they were more numerous, as was likely to be the case where eighty vessels were employed from one port, and only eighteen from the other. The people, too, at Liverpool seemed to be more hardened, or they related them with more coldness or less feeling. This may be accounted for from the greater number of those facts, as just related, the mention of which, as it was of course more frequent, occasioned them to lose their power of exciting surprise. All this I thought in my favour, as I should more easily, or with less obnoxiousness, come to the knowledge of what I wanted to obtain.

My friend William Rathbone, who had been looking out to supply me with intelligence, but who was desirous that I should not be imposed upon, and that I should get it from the fountainhead, introduced me to Mr. Norris for this purpose. Norris had been formerly a slave-captain, but had quitted the trade, and settled as a merchant in a different line of business. He was a man of quick penetration, and of good talents, which he had cultivated to advantage, and he had a pleasing address both as to speech and manners. He received me with great politeness, and offered me all the information I desired. I was with him five or six times at his own house for this purpose. The substance of his communications on these occasions I shall now put down, and I beg the reader's particular attention to it, as he will be referred to it in other parts of this work.

With respect to the produce of Africa, Mr. Norris enumerated many articles in which a new and valuable trade might be opened, of which he gave me one, namely, the black pepper from Whidàh before mentioned. This he gave me, to use his own expressions, as one argument among many others of the impolicy of the Slave Trade, which, by turning the attention of the inhabitants to the persons of one another for sale, hindered foreigners from discovering, and themselves from cultivating, many of the valuable productions of their own soil.

On the subject of procuring slaves, he gave it as his decided opinion that many of the inhabitants of Africa were kidnapped by each other, as they were travelling on the roads, or fishing in the creeks, or cultivating their little spots. Having learned their language, he had collected the fact from various quarters, but more particularly from the accounts of slaves whom he had transported in his own vessels. With respect, however, to Whidàh, many came from thence who were reduced to slavery in a different manner. The king of Dahomey, whose life (with the wars and customs of the Dahomans) he said he was then writing, and who was a very despotic prince, made no scruple of seizing his own subjects, and of selling them, if he was in want of any of the articles which the slave-vessels would afford him. The history of this prince's life he lent me afterwards to read, while it was yet in manuscript, in which I observed that he had recorded all the facts now mentioned. Indeed he made no hesitation to state them, either when we were by ourselves, or when others were in company with us. He repeated them at one time in the presence both of Mr. Cruden and Mr. Coupland. The latter was then a slave-merchant at Liverpool. He seemed to be fired at the relation of these circumstances. Unable to restrain himself longer, he entered into a defence of the trade, both as to the humanity and the policy of it; but Mr. Norris took up his arguments in both these cases, and answered them in a solid manner.

With respect to the Slave Trade as it affected the health of our seamen, Mr. Norris admitted it to be destructive; but I did not stand in need of this information, as I knew this part of the subject, in consequence of my familiarity with the muster-rolls, better than himself.

He admitted it also to be true, that they were too frequently ill-treated in this trade. A day or two after our conversation on this latter subject he brought me the manuscript journal of a voyage to Africa, which had been kept by a mate, with whom he was then acquainted. He brought it to me to read, as it might throw some light upon the subject on which we had talked last. In this manuscript various instances of cruel usage towards seamen were put down, from which it appeared that the mate, who wrote it, had not escaped himself.

At the last interview we had, he seemed to be so satisfied of the inhumanity, injustice, and impolicy of the trade, that he made me a voluntary offer of certain clauses, which he had been thinking of, and which, he believed, if put into an Act of Parliament, would judiciously effect its abolition. The offer of these clauses I embraced eagerly. He dictated them, and I wrote. I wrote them in a small book which I had then in my pocket. They were these:—

No vessel, under a heavy penalty, to supply foreigners with slaves.

Every vessel to pay to government a tax for a register on clearing out to supply our own islands with slaves.

Every such vessel to be prohibited from purchasing or bringing home any of the productions of Africa.

Every such vessel to be prohibited from bringing home a passenger, or any article of produce, from the West Indies.

A bounty to be given to every vessel trading in the natural productions of Africa. This bounty to be paid in part out of the tax arising from the registers of the slave-vessels.

Certain establishments to be made by government in Africa, in the Bananas, in the Isles de Los, on the banks of the Camaranca, and in other places, for the encouragement and support of the new trade to be substituted there.

Such then were the services, which Mr. Norris, at the request of William Rathbone, rendered me at Liverpool, during my stay there; and I have been very particular in detailing them, because I shall be obliged to allude to them, as I have before observed, on some important occasions in a future part of the work.

On going my rounds one day, I met accidentally with Captain Chaffers. This gentleman either was or had been in the West India employ. His heart had beaten in sympathy with mine, and he had greatly favoured our cause. He had seen me at Mr. Norris's, and learned my errand there. He told me he could introduce me in a few minutes, as we were then near at hand, to Captain Lace, if I chose it. Captain Lace, he said, had been long in the Slave Trade, and could give me very accurate information about it. I accepted his offer. On talking to Captain Lace, relative to the productions of Africa, he told me that mahogany grew at Calabar. He began to describe a tree of that kind, which he had seen there. This tree was from about eighteen inches to two feet in diameter, and about sixty feet high, or, as he expressed it, of the height of a tall chimney. As soon as he mentioned Calabar, a kind of horror came over me. His name became directly associated in my mind with the place. It almost instantly occurred to me, that he commanded the Edgar out of Liverpool, when the dreadful massacre there, as has been related, took place. Indeed I seemed to be so confident of it, that, attending more to my feelings than to my reason at this moment, I accused him with being concerned in it. This produced great confusion among us. For he looked incensed at Captain Chaffers, as if he had introduced me to him for this purpose. Captain Chaffers again seemed to be all astonishment that I should have known of this circumstance, and to be vexed that I should have mentioned it in such a manner. I was also in a state of trembling myself. Captain Lace could only say it was a bad business. But he never defended himself, nor those concerned in it. And we soon parted, to the great joy of us all.

Soon after this interview, I began to perceive that I was known in Liverpool, as well as the object for which I came. Mr. Coupland, the slave-merchant, with whom I had disputed at Mr. Norris's house, had given the alarm to those who were concerned in the trade, and Captain Lace, as may be now easily imagined, had spread it. This knowledge of me and of my errand was almost immediately productive of two effects, the first of which I shall now mention.

I had a private room at the King's Arms tavern, besides my bed-room, where I used to meditate and to write; but I generally dined in public. The company at dinner had hitherto varied but little as to number, and consisted of those, both from the town and country, who had been accustomed to keep up a connexion with the house. But now things were altered, and many people came to dine there daily with a view of seeing me, as if I had been some curious creature imported from foreign parts. They thought, also, they could thus have an opportunity of conversing with me. Slave-merchants and slave-captains came in among others for this purpose. I had observed this difference in the number of our company for two or three days. Dale, the master of the tavern, had observed it also, and told me in a good-natured manner, that many of these were my visitors, and that I was likely to bring him a great deal of custom. In a little time, however, things became serious; for they, who came to see me, always started the abolition of the Slave Trade as the subject for conversation. Many entered into the justification of this trade with great warmth, as if to ruffle my temper, or at any rate to provoke me to talk. Others threw out, with the same view, that men were going about to abolish it, who would have done much better if they had stayed at home. Others said they had heard of a person turned mad, who had conceived the thought of destroying Liverpool, and all its glory. Some gave as a toast, Success to the trade, and then laughed immoderately, and watched me when I took my glass to see if I would drink it. I saw the way in which things were now going, and I believed it would be proper that I should come to some fixed resolutions; such as, whether I should change my lodgings, and whether I should dine in private; and if not, what line of conduct it would become me to pursue on such occasions. With respect to changing my lodgings and dining in private, I conceived, if I were to do either of these things, that I should be showing an unmanly fear of my visiters, which they would turn to their own advantage. I conceived too, that, if I chose to go on as before, and to enter into conversation with them on the subject of the abolition of the Slave Trade, I might be able, by having such an assemblage of persons daily, to gather all the arguments which they could collect on the other side of our question, an advantage which I should one day feel in the future management of the cause. With respect to the line, which I should pursue in the case of remaining in the place of my abode and in my former habits, I determined never to start the subject of the abolition myself—never to abandon it when started—never to defend it but in a serious and dignified manner—and never to discover any signs of irritation, whatever provocation might be given me. By this determination I abided rigidly. The King's Arms became now daily the place for discussion on this subject. Many tried to insult me, but to no purpose. In all these discussions I found the great advantage of having brought Mr. Falconbridge with me from Bristol; for he was always at the table; and when my opponents, with a disdainful look, tried to ridicule my knowledge, among those present, by asking me if I had ever been on the coast of Africa myself, he used generally to reply, "But I have. I know all your proceedings there, and that his statements are true." These and other words put in by him, who was an athletic and resolute-looking man, were of great service to me. All disinterested persons, of whom there were four or five daily in the room, were uniformly convinced by our arguments, and took our part, and some of them very warmly. Day after day we beat our opponents out of the field, as many of the company acknowledged, to their no small notification, in their presence. Thus, while we served the cause by discovering all that could be said against it, we served it by giving numerous individuals proper ideas concerning it, and of interesting them in our favour.

The second effect which I experienced was, that from this time I could never get any one to come forward as an evidence to serve the cause. There were, I believe, hundreds of persons in Liverpool, and in the neighbourhood of it, who had been concerned in this traffic, and who had left it, all of whom could have given such testimony concerning it as would have insured its abolition. But none of them would now speak out. Of these, indeed, there were some, who were alive to the horrors of it, and who lamented that it should still continue. But yet even these were backward in supporting me. All that they did was just privately to see me, to tell me that I was right, and to exhort me to persevere: but as to coming forward to be examined publicly, my object was so unpopular, and would become so much more so when brought into parliament, that they would have their houses pulled down, if they should then appear as public instruments in the annihilation of the trade. With this account I was obliged to rest satisfied; nor could I deny, when I considered the spirit, which had manifested itself, and the extraordinary number of interested persons in the place, that they had some reason for their fears; and that these fears were not groundless, appeared afterwards; for Dr. Binns, a respectable physician belonging to the religious society of the Quakers, and to whom Isaac Hadwen had introduced me, was near falling into a mischievous plot, which had been laid against him, because he was one of the subscribers to the institution for the abolition of the Slave Trade, and because he was suspected of having aided me in promoting that object.

CHAPTER XVIII.

Hostile disposition towards the author increases, on account of his known patronage of the seamen employed in the Slave Trade; manner of procuring and paying them at Liverpool; their treatment and mortality.—Account of the murder of Peter Green; trouble taken by the author to trace it; his narrow escape.—Goes to Lancaster, but returns to Liverpool; leaves the latter place.

It has appeared that a number of persons used to come and see me, out of curiosity, at the King's Arms tavern; and that these manifested a bad disposition towards me, which was near breaking out into open insult. Now the cause of all this was, as I have observed, the knowledge which people had obtained relative to my errand at this place. But this hostile disposition was increased by another circumstance, which I am now to mention. I had been so shocked at the treatment of the seamen belonging to the slave-vessels at Bristol, that I determined, on my arrival at Liverpool, to institute an inquiry concerning it there also. I had made considerable progress in it, so that few seamen were landed from such vessels, but I had some communication with them; and though no one else would come near me, to give me any information about the trade, these were always forward to speak to me, and to tell me their grievances, if it were only with the hope of being able to get redress. The consequence of this was, that they used to come to the King's Arms tavern to see me. Hence, one, two, and three, were almost daily to be found about the door; and this happened quite as frequently after the hostility just mentioned had shown itself, as before. They, therefore, who came to visit me out of curiosity, could not help seeing my sailor visiters; and on inquiring into their errand, they became more than ever incensed against me.

The first result of this increased hostility towards me was an application from some of them to the master of the tavern, that he would not harbour me. This he communicated to me in a friendly manner, but he was by no means desirous that I should leave him. On the other hand, he hoped I would stay long enough to accomplish my object. I thought it right, however, to take the matter into consideration; and having canvassed it, I resolved to remain with him, for the reasons mentioned in the former chapter. But, that I might avoid doing anything that would be injurious to his interest, as well as in some measure avoid giving unnecessary offence to others, I took lodgings in Williamson Square, where I retired to write, and occasionally to sleep, and to which place all seamen, desirous of seeing me, were referred. Hence I continued to get the same information as before, but in a less obnoxious and injurious manner.

The history of the seamen employed in the slave-vessels belonging to the port of Liverpool, I found to be similar to that of those from Bristol.

They who went into this trade were of two classes. The first consisted of those who were ignorant of it, and to whom generally improper representations of advantage had been made, for the purpose of enticing them into it. The second consisted of those who, by means of a regular system, kept up by the mates and captains, had been purposely brought by their landlords into distress, from which they could only be extricated by going into this hateful employ. How many have I seen, with tears in their eyes, put into boats, and conveyed to vessels, which were then lying at the Black Rock, and which were only waiting to receive them to sail away!

The manner of paying them in the currency of the islands was the same as at Bristol. But this practice was not concealed at Liverpool, as it was at the former place. The articles of agreement were printed, so that all who chose to buy might read them. At the same time it must be observed, that seamen were never paid in this manner in any other employ; and that the African wages, though nominally higher for the sake of procuring hands, were thus made to be actually lower than in other trades.

The loss by death was so similar, that it did not signify whether the calculation on a given number was made either at this or the other port. I had, however, a better opportunity at this than I had at the other, of knowing the loss, as it related to those whose constitutions had been ruined, or who had been rendered incapable by disease, of continuing their occupation at sea. For the slave-vessels which returned to Liverpool, sailed immediately into the docks, so that I saw at once their sickly and ulcerated crews. The number of vessels, too, was so much greater from this, than from any other port, that their sick made a more conspicuous figure in the infirmary; and they were seen also more frequently in the streets.

With respect to their treatment, nothing could be worse. It seemed to me to be but one barbarous system from the beginning to the end. I do not say barbarous, as if premeditated, but it became so in consequence of the savage habits gradually formed by a familiarity with miserable sights, and with a course of action inseparable from the trade. Men in their first voyages usually disliked the traffic; and if they were happy enough then to abandon it, they usually escaped the disease of a hardened heart. But if they went a second and a third time, their disposition became gradually changed. It was impossible for them to be accustomed to carry away men and women by force, to keep them in chains, to see their tears, to hear their mournful lamentations, to behold the dead and the dying, to be obliged to keep up a system of severity amidst all this affliction,—in short, it was impossible for them to be witnesses, and this for successive voyages, to the complicated mass of misery passing in a slave-ship, without losing their finer feelings, or without contracting those habits of moroseness and cruelty which would brutalize their nature. Now, if we consider that persons could not easily become captains (and to these the barbarities were generally chargeable by actual perpetration, or by consent) till they had been two or three voyages in this employ, we shall see the reason why it would be almost a miracle, if they, who were thus employed in it, were not rather to become monsters, than to continue to be men.

While I was at Bristol, I heard from an officer of the Alfred, who gave me the intelligence privately, that the steward of a Liverpool ship, whose name was Green, had been murdered in that ship. The Alfred was in Bonny river at the same time, and his own captain, (so infamous for his cruelty, as has been before shown,) was on board when it happened. The circumstances, he said, belonging to this murder, were, if report were true, of a most atrocious nature, and deserved to be made the subject of inquiry. As to the murder itself, he observed, it had passed as a notorious and uncontradicted fact.

This account was given me just as I had made an acquaintance with Mr. Falconbridge, and I informed him of it; he said he had no doubt of its truth; for in his last voyage he went to Bonny himself, where the ship was then lying, in which the transaction happened: the king and several of the black traders told him of it. The report then current was simply this, that the steward had been barbarously beaten one evening; that after this he was let down with chains upon him into a boat, which was alongside of the ship, and that the next morning he was found dead. On my arrival at Liverpool, I resolved to inquire into the truth of this report. On looking into one of the wet docks, I saw the name of the vessel alluded to; I walked over the decks of several others, and got on board her. Two people were walking up and down her, and one was leaning upon a rail by the side. I asked the latter how many slaves this ship had carried in her last voyage; he replied he could not tell; but one of the two persons walking about could answer me, as he had sailed out and returned in her. This man came up to us, and joined in conversation. He answered my questions and many others, and would have shown me the ship, but on asking him how many seamen had died on the voyage, he changed his manner, and said, with apparent hesitation, that he could not tell. I asked him next, what had become, of the steward Green. He said he believed he was dead. I asked how the seamen had been used. He said, not worse than others. I then asked whether Green had been used worse than others. He replied, he did not then recollect. I found that he was now quite upon his guard, and as I could get no satisfactory answer from him I left the ship.

On the next day I looked over the muster-roll of this vessel; on examining it, I found that sixteen of the crew had died; I found also the name of Peter Green; I found, again, that the latter had been put down among the dead. I observed, also, that the ship had left Liverpool on the 5th of June, 1786, and had returned on the 5th of June, 1787, and that Peter Green was put down as having died on the 19th of September; from all which circumstances it was evident that he must, as my Bristol informant asserted, have died upon the Coast.

Notwithstanding this extraordinary coincidence of name, mortality, time, and place, I could gain no further intelligence about the affair till within about ten days before I left Liverpool; when among the seamen, who came to apply to me in Williamson Square was George Ormond. He came to inform me of his own ill-usage; from which circumstance I found that he had sailed in the same ship with Peter Green. This led me to inquire into the transaction in question, and I received from him the following account.

Peter Green had been shipped as steward. A black woman, of the name of Rodney, went out in the same vessel; she belonged to the owners of it, and was to be an interpretess to the slaves who should be purchased. About five in the evening, some time in the month of September, the vessel then lying in Bonny river, the captain, as was his custom, went on shore. In his absence,

Rodney, the black woman, asked Green for the keys of the pantry, which he refused her, alleging that the captain had already beaten him for having given them to her on a former occasion, when she drank the wine. The woman, being passionate, struck him, and a scuffle ensued, out of which Green extricated himself as well as he could.

When the scuffle was over the woman retired to the cabin, and appeared pensive. Between eight and nine in the evening, the captain, who was attended by the captain of the Alfred, came on board; Rodney immediately ran to him, and informed him that Green had made an assault upon her. The captain, without any inquiry, beat him severely, and ordered his hands to be made fast to some bolts on the starboard side of the ship and under the half deck, and then flogged him himself, using the lashes of the cat-of-nine-tails upon his back at one time, and the double walled knot at the end of it upon his head at another; and stopping to rest at intervals, and using each hand alternately, that he might strike with the greater severity.

The pain had now become so very severe, that Green cried out, and entreated the captain of the Alfred, who was standing by, to pity his hard case, and to intercede for him. But the latter replied, that he would have served me in the same manner. Unable to find a friend here, he called upon the chief mate; but this only made matters worse, for the captain then ordered the latter to flog him also; which he did for some time, using however only the lashes of the instrument. Green then called in his distress upon the second mate to speak for him; but the second mate was immediately ordered to perform the same cruel office, and was made to persevere in it till the lashes were all worn into threads. But the barbarity did not close here; for the captain, on seeing the instrument now become useless, ordered another, with which he flogged him as before, beating him at times over the head with the double-walled knot, and changing his hands, and cursing his own left hand for not being able to strike so severe a blow as his right.

The punishment, as inflicted by all parties, had now lasted two hours and a half, when George Ormond was ordered to cut down one of the arms, and the boatswain the other, from the places of their confinement; this being done, Green lay motionless on the deck. He attempted to utter something, Ormond understood it to be the word water; but no water was allowed him. The captain, on the other hand, said he had not yet done with him, and ordered him to be confined with his arms across, his right hand to his left foot, and his left hand to his right foot. For this purpose the carpenter brought shackles, and George Ormond was compelled to put them on. The captain then ordered some tackle to be made fast to the limbs of the said Peter Green, in which situation he was then hoisted up, and afterwards let down into a boat, which was lying alongside the ship. Michael Cunningham was then sent to loose the tackle, and to leave him there.

In the middle watch, or between one and two next morning, George Ormond looked out of one of the port-holes, and called to Green, but received no answer. Between two and three, Paul Berry, a seaman, was sent down into the boat, and found him dead. He made his report to one of the officers of the ship. About five in the morning the body was brought up, and laid on the waist near the half-deck door. The captain on seeing the body when he rose, expressed no concern, but ordered it to be knocked out of irons, and to be buried at the usual place of interment for seamen, or Bonny Point. I may now observe, that the deceased was in good health before the punishment took place, and in high spirits; for he played upon the flute only a short time before Rodney asked him for the keys, while those seamen, who were in health, danced.

On hearing this cruel relation from George Ormond, who was throughout a material witness to the scene, I had no doubt in my own mind of the truth of it; but I thought it right to tell him at once that I had seen a person, about four weeks ago, who had been the same voyage with him and Peter Green, but yet who had no recollection of these circumstances. Upon this he looked quite astonished, and began to grow angry; he maintained he had seen the whole; he had also held the candle himself during the whole punishment. He asserted that one candle and half of another were burnt out while it lasted. He said also that, while the body lay in the waist, he had handled the abused parts, and had put three of his fingers into a hole, made by the double walled knot, in the head, from whence a quantity of blood and, he believed, brains issued. He then challenged me to bring the man, before him; I desired him upon this to be cool, and to come to me the next day, and I would then talk with him again upon the subject.

In the interim I consulted the muster-roll of the vessel again; I found the name of George Ormond; he had sailed in her out of Liverpool, and had been discharged at the latter end of January in the West Indies, as he had told me. I found also the names of Michael Cunningham and of Paul Berry, whom he had mentioned. It was obvious also that Ormond's account of the captain of the Alfred being on board at the time of the punishment tallied with that given me at Bristol by an officer of that vessel, and that his account of letting down Peter Green into the boat tallied with that which Mr. Falconbridge, as I mentioned before, had heard from the king and the black traders in Bonny river.

When he came to me next day, he came in high spirits. He said he had found out the man whom I had seen. The man, however, when he talked to him about the murder of Peter Green, acknowledged every thing concerning it. Ormond intimated that this man was to sail again in the same ship under the promise of being an officer, and that he had been kept on board, and had been enticed to a second voyage, for no other purpose than that he might be prevented from divulging the matter. I then asked Ormond, whether he thought the man would acknowledge the murder in my hearing. He replied, "that, if I were present, he thought he would not say much about it, as he was soon to be under the same captain, but that he would not deny it. If, however, I were out of sight, though I might be in hearing, he believed he would acknowledge the facts."

By the assistance of Mr. Falconbridge, I found a public-house, which had two rooms in it: nearly at the top of the partition between them was a small window, which a person might look through by standing upon a chair. I desired Ormond, one evening, to invite the man into the larger room, in which he was to have a candle, and, to talk with him on the subject. I proposed to station myself in the smallest in the dark, so that by looking through the window I could both see and hear him, and yet be unperceived myself. The room, in which I was to be, was one where the dead were frequently carried to be owned. We were all in our places at the time appointed. I directly discovered that it was the same man with whom I had conversed on board the ship in the wet docks. I heard him distinctly relate many of the particulars of the murder, and acknowledge them all. Ormond, after having talked with him some time, said, "Well, then, you believe Peter Green was actually murdered?" He replied, "If Peter Green was not murdered, no man ever was." What followed I do not know. I had heard quite enough; and the room was so disagreeable in smell, that I did not choose to stay in it longer than was absolutely necessary.

I own I was now quite satisfied that the murder had taken place, and my first thought was to bring the matter before the mayor, and to take up three of the officers of the ship. But, in mentioning my intention to my friends, I was dissuaded from it. They had no doubt but that in Liverpool, as there was now a notion that the Slave Trade would become a subject of parliamentary inquiry, every, effort would be made to overthrow me. They were of opinion also that such of the magistrates, as were interested in the trade, when applied to for warrants of apprehension, would contrive to give notice to the officers to escape. In addition to this they believed, that so many in the town were already incensed against me, that I should be torn to pieces, and the house where I lodged burnt down, if I were to make the attempt. I thought it right therefore to do nothing for the present; but I sent Ormond to London, to keep him out of the way of corruption, till I should make up my mind as to further proceedings on the subject. It is impossible, if I observe the bounds I have prescribed myself, and I believe the reader will be glad of it on account of his own feelings, that I should lay open the numerous cases, which came before me at Liverpool, relative to the ill-treatment of the seamen in this wicked trade. It may be sufficient to say, that they harassed my constitution, and affected my spirits daily. They were in my thoughts on my pillow after I retired to rest, and I found them before my eyes when I awoke. Afflicting, however, as they were, they were of great use in the promotion of our cause: for they served, whatever else failed, as a stimulus to perpetual energy: they made me think light of former labours, and they urged me imperiously to new. And here I may observe, that among the many circumstances which ought to excite our joy on considering the great event of the abolition of the Slave Trade, which has now happily taken place, there are few for which we ought to be more grateful, than that from this time our commerce ceases to breed such abandoned wretches: while those, who have thus been bred in it, and who may yet find employment in other trades, will, in the common course of nature, be taken off in a given time, so that our marine will at length be purified from a race of monsters, which have helped to cripple its strength, and to disgrace its character.

The temper of many of the interested people of Liverpool had now become still more irritable, and their hostility more apparent than before. I received anonymous letters, entreating me to leave it, or I should otherwise never leave it alive. The only effect which this advice had upon me, was to make me more vigilant when I went out at night. I never stirred out at this time without Mr. Falconbridge; and he never accompanied me without being well armed. Of this, however, I knew nothing until we had left the place. There was certainly a time when I had reason to believe that I had a narrow escape. I was one day on the pier-head with many others looking at some little boats below at the time of a heavy gale. Several persons, probably out of curiosity, were hastening thither. I had seen all I intended to see, and was departing, when I noticed eight or nine persons making towards me. I was then only about eight or nine yards from the precipice of the pier, but going from it. I expected that they would have divided to let me through them; instead of which they closed upon me and bore me back. I was borne within a yard of the precipice, when I discovered my danger; and perceiving among them the murderer of Peter Green, and two others who had insulted me at the King's Arms, it instantly struck me that they had a design to throw me over the pier-head; which they might have done at this time, and yet have pleaded that I had been killed by accident. There was not a moment to lose. Vigorous on account of the danger, I darted forward. One of them, against whom I pushed myself, fell down: their ranks were broken; and I escaped, not without blows, amidst their imprecations and abuse.

I determined now to go to Lancaster, to make some inquiries about the Slave Trade there. I had a letter of introduction to William Jepson, one of the religious society of the Quakers, for this purpose. I found from him, that, though there were slave-merchants at Lancaster, they made their outfits at Liverpool, as a more convenient port. I learnt too from others, that the captain of the last vessel, which had sailed out of Lancaster to the coast of Africa for slaves, had taken off so many of the natives treacherously, that any other vessel known to come from it would be cut off. There were only now one or two superannuated captains living in the place. Finding I could get no oral testimony, I was introduced into the Custom-house. Here I just looked over the muster-rolls of such slave-vessels as had formerly sailed from this port; and having found that the loss of seamen was precisely in the same proportion as elsewhere, I gave myself no further trouble, but left the place.

On my return to Liverpool, I was informed by Mr. Falconbridge, that a ship-mate of Ormond, of the name of Patrick Murray, who had been discharged in the West Indies, had arrived there. This man, he said, had been to call upon me in my absence, to seek redress for his own bad usage; but in the course of conversation he had confirmed all the particulars as stated by Ormond, relative to the murder of Peter Green. On consulting the muster-roll of the ship, I found his name, and that he had been discharged in the West Indies on the 2nd of February. I determined, therefore, to see him. I cross-examined him in the best manner I could. I could neither make him contradict himself, nor say anything that militated against the testimony of Ormond. I was convinced, therefore, of the truth of the transaction; and, having obtained his consent, I sent him to London to stay with the latter, till he should hear further from me. I learnt also from Mr. Falconbridge, that visitors had continued to come to the King's Arms during my absence; that they had been very liberal of their abuse of me; and that one of them did not hesitate to say (which is remarkable) that "I deserved to be thrown over the pierhead." Finding now that I could get no further evidence; that the information which I had already obtained was considerable[A]; and that the committee had expressed an earnest desire, in a letter which I had received, that I would take into consideration the propriety of writing my Essay on the *Impolicy of the Slave Trade* as soon as possible, I determined upon leaving Liverpool.

[A]: In London, Bristol, and Liverpool, I had already obtained the names of more than 20,000 seamen, in different voyages, knowing what had become of each.

I went round accordingly and took leave of my friends. The last of these was William Rathbone, and I have to regret, that it was also the last time I ever saw him. Independently of the gratitude I owed him for assisting me in this great cause, I respected him highly as a man: he possessed a fine understanding with a solid judgment: he was a person of extraordinary simplicity of manners. Though he lived in a state of pecuniary independence, he gave an example of great temperance, as well as of great humility of mind: but however humble he appeared, he had always the courage to dare to do that which was right, however it might resist the customs or the prejudices of men. In his own line of trade, which was that of a timber-merchant on an extensive scale, he would not allow any article to be sold for the use of a slave-ship, and he always refused those, who applied to him for materials for such purposes. But it is evident that it was his intention, if he had lived, to bear his testimony still more publicly upon this subject; for an advertisement, stating the ground of his refusal to furnish anything for this traffic upon Christian principles, with a memorandum for two advertisements in the Liverpool papers, was found among his papers at his decease.

CASE STUDIES

The Case and Southworth records

The Case and Southworth records (380 MD 33-36) cover the years from 1754 to 1769. They are the surviving commercial manuscripts of a Liverpool merchant firm with a branch house in Kingston, Jamaica. Thomas Case was listed in the Liverpool trade directory for 1766 as a merchant in Water Street. He owned a number of ships, became a member of the African Company of Liverpool, and held shares in eighteen slaving vessels. Two of these ships, the Fortune and the Bee, were vessels where he was the sole owner; the others were co-owned

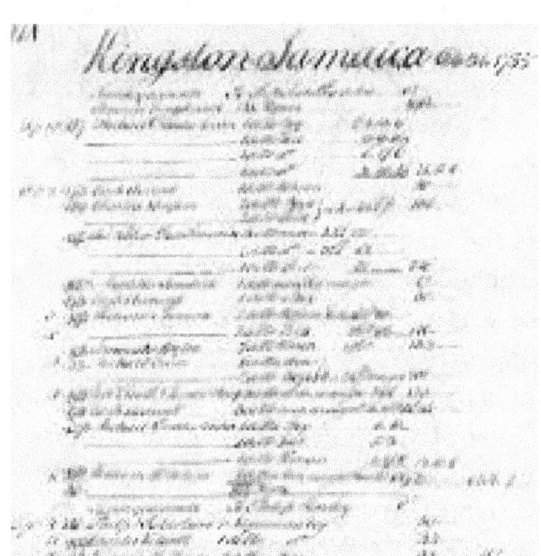

with his brother Clayton and other Liverpool merchants such as William Boats and William Davenport. Thomas Case entered into an insurance brokerage business with William Gregson in 1774. This was dissolved in 1778, however, when bankruptcy proceedings were issued against Case after he fell into financial difficulties. Nicholas Southworth, who managed the Kingston end of the Case & Southworth partnership, had captained three slaving vessels from Liverpool to Africa and the Caribbean in 1746, 1748 and 1752. Southworth was the part owner of several slave vessels in the 1750s and 1760s but he never co-owned vessels with Case. The partnership of Case & Southworth appears to have flourished until the records end in 1767.

The records of Case & Southworth are bound volumes with detailed information on the import of hardware, textiles and provisions from British and Irish merchants via Liverpool to Kingston; the sale of lots of slaves in Kingston; and imports of sugar, rum, pimento and wood at Liverpool. Both ends of the business, at Liverpool and Kingston, acted on commission, but sales were much more valuable at the Jamaican end (largely owing to the slave sales) than on Merseyside. The Liverpool house under Case sold on behalf of far fewer people than the Kingston branch under Southworth. This resulted from the much larger population of the Lancashire port and its hinterland compared with the much smaller white population in Jamaica. The Account Book (380 MD 33) and the Journal (380 MD 34) include a mass of daily transactions. At first sight these list a bewildering array of sales but they can be collated and analysed to indicate some interesting patterns in consumer behaviour. Some of the detailed accounts of slave sales, giving the purchasers, date of purchase, size of lot sold and prices gained, are duplicated in the two Sales account books (380 MD 35-36) but some are not. The Case and Southworth account books are some of the most detailed sales' records of Africans in the British slave trade available in any British archive.

CASE STUDIES

The Thomas Leyland records

Thomas Leyland (c.1752-1827) was a merchant, banker, millionaire and three times Mayor of Liverpool. In 1766 he won a lottery prize of £20,000, which he used to build up his business affairs. He was involved in various trading partnerships. He built up much of his mercantile

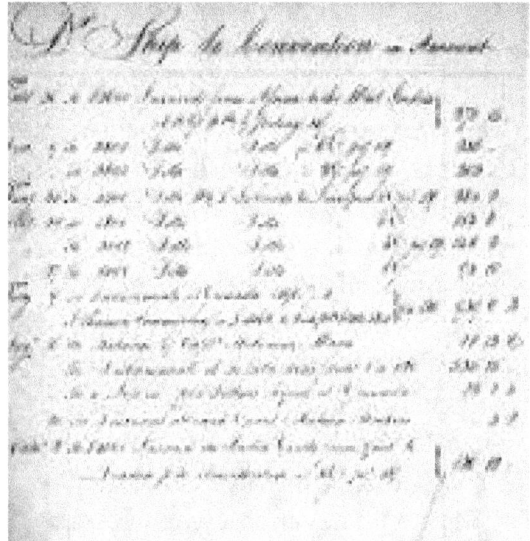

fortune from participation in the slave trade, and was particularly active in that traffic as well in various other trades in the last two decades of the eighteenth century. Leyland had an interest in sixty-nine slaving voyages from Liverpool. The ships in which he was concerned delivered an estimated 22,365 Africans to the Americas. He was associated with some other important Liverpool merchants but he also linked up with smaller fry. Thus, for example, he was part owner with David Tuohy in the slave ship Kitty in 1789. In 1802 Leyland entered into a banking partnership with Clarke and Roscoe, a firm of Liverpool bankers. After this was dissolved in 1806, he set up his own bank in Liverpool with his nephew Richard Bullin in 1807.

Through amalgamations, his banking business later became part of the Midland (now HSBC) Bank. Thomas Leyland left a fortune of £600,000 in 1827, making him one of the wealthiest decedents in Britain at the time. In addition to the records made available here, further documents relating to Leyland's slave trading and banking career survive in the HSBC archives and among the Dumbell Papers at Liverpool University Library. A good many of Leyland's ships' books relating to the slave trade were unfortunately destroyed by bomb damage during the Second World War.

Case Studies sourced from: https://www.britishonlinearchives.co.uk

CASE STUDIES

The Tuohy papers

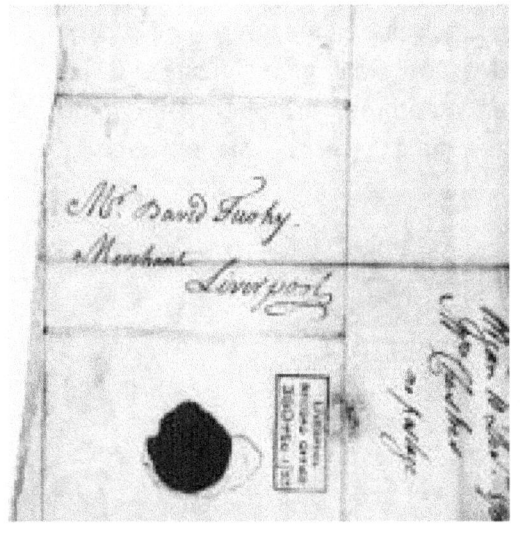

The documents pertaining to David Tuohy are those of an Irishman who spent fourteen years in the African trade, including the captaincy of four slave voyages between 1765 and 1769 and part-ownership of ten Liverpool slave ships from 1772 to 1786. Tuohy married in Liverpool in 1768 and settled there in 1771. After his experience as a captain of slave vessels, he settled down as a merchant on Merseyside. In Gore's Liverpool Directory for 1781, he is described as a merchant resident at 48 Old Hall Street. His correspondence indicates that he divided his commercial affairs mainly between trade between Liverpool and Ireland, a trade in which he imported beef, butter and tallow, and exported salt, beer and cheese, and the slave trade. He participated in voyages where he could spread his investment among other partners, as in the voyage of the Brig Nancy in 1774 in which he held a one-sixth share (380 TUO/4/7). His ventures in the triangular slave trade involved sending ships to the Windward, Ivory and Gold coasts, the Bight of Benin, and especially Angola, and then selling the Africans at Jamaica, Barbados, St. Kitts, Antigua, Dominica and Grenada. Tuohy had few mercantile contacts on the North American continent apart from in Charleston, South Carolina. He probably died in the late 1780s or early 1790s; the last mention of him in these papers is a letter addressed to him dated September 1788 (380 TUO/6/4).

Case Studies sourced from: https://www.britishonlinearchives.co.uk

CASE STUDIES

John Tomlinson

John Tomlinson's Account Current with John Knight covers shares in slave vessels between 1757 and 1777. Tomlinson was the first owner of thirty Liverpool slaving voyages that disembarked some 5,900 slaves to markets in North America and the Caribbean. Though little contemporary material has survived about Knight, he was a major Liverpool slave trader with an interest in 111 voyages over thirty years (1744-74)

Case Studies sourced from: https://www.britishonlinearchives.co.uk

Liverpool Mayors During the Slave Trade Period

William Clayton – Liverpool Mayor

(after 1650 – 7 July 1715) was an English merchant and politician from Liverpool.

Clayton was from Preston, but followed his uncle Thomas Clayton to Liverpool, where he became a successful tobacco and sugar merchant. He was Mayor of Liverpool from 1689 to 1690, and then became an alderman of the city.

In the Parliament of England, he served as a Member of Parliament (MP) for Liverpool from 1698 to 1708. After the Union with Scotland, he was elected as a Liverpool MP to the new House of Commons of Great Britain from 1713 to 1715.

Bryan Blundell – Liverpool Mayor

A philanthropist and captain of 'The Mulberry' ship which transported a large number of slaves to Virginia, and was also the first ship to dock in the New Dock in Liverpool. Blundell is however most noted for the foundation of The Liverpool Blue Coat Hospital School in 1708, which was established by Blundell and his close friend, the Reverend Robert Stythe, the rector of Liverpool, to provide an education for orphans in Liverpool. Blundell also served twice as the Lord Mayor of Liverpool in between 1721 and 1722 and 1728 and 1729, a position also held by his son Henry Blundell and his grandson Henry Blundell-Hollinshead.

James Clemens - Liverpool Mayor

(fl. 1750-1775) was a Liverpool, England merchant and shipowner, and Lord Mayor of Liverpool.

Clemens made three voyages to Angola in the 1750s, in addition to other slave runs, in 1767 he sent the Ranger under William Speers to acquire slaves in Angola and take them to Barbados. Also in 1767 he became a member of the town council of Liverpool, and was, from 1775-6, the Lord Mayor. While Lord Mayor he presented St Pauls, Stoneycroft with a two cwt (104 kg) bell.

Thomas Smyth - Liverpool Mayor

(1737? – 1824) was an English merchant, banker and Lord Mayor of Liverpool. Smyth became bankrupt in 1793, when the bank failed, hit by the fall in the price of cotton at the outbreak of the French Revolutionary Wars. Losing most of his possessions, Smyth was able to remain at Fair View, Toxteth Park, by arrangement with his landlord William Roe, son of Charles Roe. An estate in Macclesfield, that had come through his wife, remained unaffected. The impact in Liverpool of the failure of Charles Caldwell & Co. was serious on business confidence, and there was a failed attempt to obtain a loan from the Bank of England. The Corporation resolved the financial crisis by an Act of Parliament allowing it to issue banknotes. Smyth died, aged 87, at Fence House in Macclesfield, on 12 July 1824.

Most Liverpool Mayors Had A Financial Interest In Slavery / Directly Or Indirectly

1786–87 James Gildart, the Younger
1787–88 Thomas Earle
1788–89 James Blackburne, the Younger
1789–90 Thomas Smyth
1790–91 John Sparling
1791–92 Henry Blundell
1792–93 Clayton Tarleton
1793–94 Henry Blundell
1794–95 John Shaw
1795–96 Peter Baker
1976 Thomas Naylor
1796–97 George Dunbar
1797–98 Thomas Staniforth
1798–99 Thomas Leyland
1799–1800 Pudsey Dawson
1800–01 John Shaw
1801–02 Peter Whitfield Brancker
1802–03 Jonas Bold
1803–04 William Harper
1804 John Bridge Aspinall
1804–05 William Harper
1805–06 Henry Clay
1806–07 Thomas Molyneux

Web Source: https://en.wikipedia.org/wiki/Lord_Mayor_of_Liverpool

Web Source: http://www.recoveredhistories.org/storiesproslavery.php

Liverpool Street Names: the Slavery Connection

Liverpool street names have in the past become a contentious issue , due to the fact that many commemorate individuals who prospered from the slave trade. In this article we will look at some of those streets – and how it was that they came to have places and streets named after them. Some believe that streets were not named after people because they were slavers. They were honoured in this way because they were landowners, decision makers, politicians, patrons of the arts and powerful business people. Here are a few of the streets...

Bold Street

Bold Street with the Lyceum and St Lukes at the top of the street

Bold Street is named after Jonas Bold, who originally leased the land from Liverpool Corporation in around 1785-6. He also owned the plot at the top of the street, which is now the site of St Luke's Church. At the bottom of Bold Street is the Lyceum Club, built by the architect Thomas Harrison and opened in 1802. It was built to house the Liverpool Library, which is thought to be the oldest public subscription library in the country. Many of the founder members of the Lyceum traded in enslaved Africans. Prior to Bold acquiring the land it had been home to the rope-works of the slave traders Joseph and Jonathan Brooks, hence the area using the Rope – walks title today.

Blackburne Place

Blackburne House - Blackburn Place

Blackburn Place in Liverpool 8, is named after John Blackburne, (1693-1786) Originally from Orford near Warrington, John Blackburne was a slave trader who is named on the list of merchants trading with Africa in 1752. His father John Blackburne senior served as mayor of Liverpool in 1760 and was an active member of the town's elite. Blackburne made a fortune in Liverpool and used some of his wealth to refurbish Orford Hall. In addition to slave trading he was a salt merchant who owned the salt works adjacent to Liverpool's second wet dock, which opened in 1753. Originally it was named the South Dock, but due to the proximity of Blackburne's salt works it quickly became known as the Salthouse Dock. Blackburne was also an investor in canal building; many Liverpool slave traders invested their money in other interests to take advantage of industries springing up around southern Lancashire. These included salt manufacture, banking, shipbuilding, rope-making and coal mining.

Clarence Street

Named after the Duke of Clarence, later William IV. He visited Liverpool in 1790 when Clarence Street was laid. The Duke was very popular in Liverpool because he spoke in the House of Lords in favour of the slave trade. In 1799, in recognition of his services, the Freedom of the Borough was conferred on him.

Cropper Street

Cropper Street was named after James Cropper (1773–1840), a merchant and philanthropist, he moved from Winstanley to Liverpool at the age of 17 and was apprenticed to the Rathbone Brothers, the first Liverpool merchants importing cotton from America. He later established his own company Cropper, Benson & Co, and his business proved to be a highly prosperous one, and the wealth generated from it enabled Cropper to engage in a number of religious and philanthropic activities. The main focus of his attention was the campaign for the abolition of slavery; he wrote pamphlets and sent them to William Wilberforce at an early stage in the anti-slavery campaign. His activities however were very unpopular in Liverpool and many of the West India merchants who owned plantations in the Caribbean were critical of him. In 1823–4 he was subject to a series of attacks in the columns of the Liverpool newspapers by Sir John Gladstone,

Cunliffe Street

Named after Foster Cunliffe, an enterprising and successful merchant and slave trader who was Mayor in 1716, 1729 and 1735. Inscribed on his monument in St Peter's Church were the words: 'a merchant whose sagacity, honesty and diligence procured wealth and credit to himself and his country; a magistrate who administered justice with discernment, candour and impartiality, a Christian devout and exemplary.'

Dorans Lane

Felix Doran was an Irish merchant   who lived in Lord Street. He was   part-owner of the slave ship `Bloom'   and he shared in the profit of £28123   from the sale of 307 slaves on one voyage alone.

Earle St

NAMED after the Earle family who were slave traders throughout the eighteenth century. John Earle and his two sons Ralph and Thomas served on the town council and all three held the office of mayor

Gildart St

NAMED after Richard Gildart who was a slave trader and a politician. He was listed among the Company of Merchants trading to Africa in 1752. At that time he owned three ships involved in the slave trade. Gildart served on the town council, was mayor three times, a bailiff and MP for the town from 1734 to 1754.

Goree

Goree was a bare basalt rock off Cape Verde where slaves were gathered together for shipment to the plantations.

Great Newton Street

Named after John Newton, once the master of a ship engaged in the slave trade who became a Church of England clergyman. In cooperation with the poet William Cowper, he wrote the Olney hymns, of which the best known is `Amazing Grace'.

Lord Nelson Street

Named after Admiral Horatio Nelson (17S8-1805), England's greatest naval hero. He was a great favourite with Liverpudlians because, in addition to his professional success, he supported the slave trade. In 1798, he was conferred with the Freedom of the Borough. In acknowledging the honour, he wrote from the `Victory': `I was taught to appreciate the value of our West India possessions, nor   shall their interests be infringed while I have an arm to fight in their defence.'

New Bird Street

Named after Alderman Joseph Bird. a slave trader, who was Mayor in 1746. A street between James Street and Redcross Street had been named in his honour but it was abolished in the l8th century and New Bird Street was named in replacement.

Oldham Street

It was named after Captain James Oldham, who built the first house in the street. He was engaged in the   Middle Passage, the Africa to West Indies section of the triangular route followed by the slave traders. Oldham died at sea in 1825.

Park Lane

MANY merchants' warehouses were situated in this area. Charles Roe & Company, in nearby Sparling Street, was founded in 1767 and supplied copper and brass goods and equipment, including manillas, for trading in Africa. Many black seamen lived in the area in the nineteenth century.

Rodney St

BUILT between about 1782 and 1801 this street provided homes for many of Liverpool's elite merchants and the buildings still reflect that wealth. It was named after Admiral Rodney who defeated the French in St Lucia on 1782 to preserve British influence in the West Indies. Rodney supported the slave trade. John Gladstone, father of prime minister William Ewart Gladstone, lived on Rodney Street. He made his wealth through the sugar plantations in Demerara and Jamaica.

Tarleton St

NAMED after a vigorous slaving family in Liverpool for over three generations. Three of John Tarleton's sons were involved in the trade between 1786 and 1788 and had shares in 52 slaving voyages. The fourth son Banastre was an MP and an opponent of abolition.

The Athenaeum

FOUNDED in 1799 as a gentlemen's club, library and reading room by a group which included abolitionists William Roscoe and James Currie.

Town Hall

IT WAS built in the 1750s and rebuilt after a fire in 1795. The frieze around the outside, illustrating Liverpool's trading routes, include lions, crocodiles, elephants and African faces. The hall was paid for partly by wealth amassed through the slave trade.

Web Source: http://www.liverpoolecho.co.uk/news/liverpool-news/story-citys-past-written-stone-3505844

TRUE STORIES OF THE HORRORS OF SLAVERY

TRUE STORIES OF THE HORRORS OF SLAVERY

Margaret Garner

Margaret Garner

Margaret Garner (called Peggy) was an enslaved African-American woman in pre-Civil War America who was notorious – or celebrated – for killing her own daughter rather than allowing the child to be returned to slavery. She and her family had escaped in January 1856 across the frozen Ohio River to Cincinnati, but they were apprehended by U. S. Marshals acting under the Fugitive Slave Act of 1850. Margaret Garner's defense attorney moved to have her tried for murder in Ohio, to be able to get a trial in a free state and to challenge the Fugitive Slave Law as well.

Her story was the inspiration for the novel Beloved (1987) by Nobel Prize winner Toni Morrison, which was adapted into a film of the same name starring Oprah Winfrey, as well as for her libretto for the early 21st-century opera Margaret Garner (2005), composed by Richard Danielpour.

On January 28, 1856, Robert and a pregnant Margaret, together with family members, escaped and fled to Cincinnati, Ohio, along with several other slave families. Robert had stolen his master's horses and sleigh along with his gun. Seventeen people were reported to have been in their party. In the coldest winter in 60 years, the Ohio River had frozen. The group crossed the ice just west of Covington, Kentucky at daybreak, and escaped to Cincinnati, then divided to avoid detection.

Robert and Margaret and their four children, with Robert's father Simon and his wife Mary, made their way to a former slave, Margaret's Uncle Joe Kite, who lived along Mill Creek, below Cincinnati. The other nine slaves in their party reached safe houses in Cincinnati and eventually escaped via the Underground Railroad to Canada. Kite went to abolitionist Levi Coffin for advice on how to get the group to safety. Coffin agreed to help them escape the city, and told Kite to take the Garner group further west of the city, where many free blacks lived, and to wait until night.

Slave catchers and U.S. Marshals found the Garners barricaded inside Kite's house before he returned. They surrounded the property, then stormed the house. Robert Garner fired several shots and wounded at least one deputy marshal. Margaret killed her two-year-old daughter with a butcher knife rather than see the child returned to slavery. She had wounded her other children, preparing to kill them and herself, when she was subdued by the posse.

The entire group was taken to jail. The subsequent trial lasted for two weeks, after which the judge deliberated another two weeks. It was "the longest and most complicated case of its kind." A typical fugitive slave hearing would have lasted less than a day. The core issue was whether the Garners would be tried as persons, and charged with the murder of their daughter, or tried as property under the Fugitive Slave Law. The defense attorney argued that Ohio's right to protect its citizens should take precedence. The slave catchers and owner argued for the precedence of federal law over the state.

The defense attempted to prove that Margaret had been liberated under a former law covering slaves taken into free states for other work. Her attorney proposed that she be charged with murder so that the case would be tried in a free state (understanding that the governor would later pardon her). The prosecuting attorney argued that the federal Fugitive Slave Law took precedence over state murder charges. Over a thousand people turned out each day to watch the proceedings, lining the streets outside the courthouse. Five hundred men were deputized to maintain order in the town.

The presiding judge Pendery ruled that Federal fugitive warrants had supervening authority. Defense attorney John Jolliffe then tried a strategy of arguing that the Fugitive Slave Act violated the guarantee of religious freedom, by compelling citizens to participate in evil by returning slaves. In the end, Pendery rejected this argument.

On the closing day of the trial, the antislavery activist Lucy Stone took the stand to defend her earlier conversations with Margaret (the prosecution had complained.) She spoke about the interracial sexual relationship that underlay part of the case:

Recalling to everyone's memory the faces of Margaret's children, and of A. K. Gaines, Stone told the packed courtroom: "The faded faces of the Negro children tell too plainly to what degradation the female slaves submit. Rather than give her daughter to that life, she killed it. If in her deep maternal love she felt the impulse to send her child back to God, to save it from coming woe, who shall say she had no right not to do so?"

Margaret Garner's actions were driven by her master's abuse and the well known abuse slaves faced nationwide. Women were known to practice infanticide to alleviate the burden of slavery from their children, however in Garner's case her children faced even more opposition due to their being born as mulattos. Mulattoes were seen as a threat as well as a disgrace among the plantation and white families, because the birth of mulatto children highlighted infidelity within the slave owning families. They reminded the family of a perceived sin, and were often beaten or sold. Garner underwent drastic measures to protect her child not only from the cruelty of the institution of slavery, but from the double threat, due to the child's mulatto status.

Margaret Garner was not immediately tried for murder, but was forced to return to a slave state along with Robert and their youngest child, a daughter of about nine months old. When Ohio authorities got an extradition warrant for Garner to try her for murder, they were unable to find her for the arrest. Archibald K. Gaines, her owner, kept moving her between cities in Kentucky. Ohio officials missed finding Margaret in Covington by a few hours, missed getting her again in Frankfort, and finally caught up with her master in Louisville, only to discover that he had put the slaves on a boat headed for his brother's plantation in Arkansas.

The Liberator reported on March 11, 1856, that the steamboat Henry Lewis, on which the Garners were being transported, began to sink after colliding with another boat. Margaret Garner and her baby daughter were thrown overboard during the collision. The baby drowned. It was reported that Margaret was happy that her baby had died and that she tried to drown herself. She and Robert were kept in Arkansas only a short time before being sent to Gaines' family friends in New Orleans as a household servant. The Garners then disappeared from sight.

In 1870 a reporter from The Cincinnati Chronicle found Robert Garner and gathered more about his life. Robert and Margaret Garner had worked in New Orleans, and in 1857 were sold to Judge Dewitt Clinton Bonham for plantation labor at Tennessee Landing, Mississippi. Robert said Margaret had died in 1858 of typhoid fever, in an epidemic in the valley. He said that before she died, Margaret urged him to "never marry again in slavery, but to live in hope of freedom."

Source: Wikipedia

TRUE STORIES OF THE HORRORS OF SLAVERY

Celia

A Slave, Trial (1855):

An Account

by

Douglas O. Linder (2011)

Celia

For nineteen-year-old Celia, a slave on a Missouri farm, five years of being repeatedly raped by her middle-aged owner was enough. On the night of June 23, 1855, she would later tell a reporter, "the Devil got into me" and Celia fatally clubbed her master as he approached her in her cabin. The murder trial of the slave Celia, coming at a time when the controversy over the issue of slavery reached new heights, raised fundamental questions about the rights of slaves to fight back against the worst of slavery's abuses.

Background and the Crime

Around 1820, Robert Newsom and his family left Virginia and headed west, finally settling land along the Middle River in southern Callaway County, Missouri. By 1850 (according to the census), Newsom owned eight-hundred acres of land and livestock that included horses, milk cows, beef cattle, hogs, sheep, and two oxen. Like the majority of Callaway County farmers, Newsom also owned slaves--five male slaves as of 1850.

During the summer of 1850, Newsom purchased from a slave owner in neighboring Audrain County a sixth slave, a fourteen-year-old girl named Celia. Shortly after returning with Celia to his farm, Newsom raped her. For female slaves, rape was an "ever present threat" and, far too often, a reality. Over the next five years, Newsom would make countless treks to Celia's slave cabin, located in a grove of fruit trees some distance from his main house, and demand sex from the teenager he considered his concubine. Celia gave birth to two children between 1851 and 1855, the second being the son of Robert Newsom.

Sometime before 1855, a real lover, another one of Newsom's slaves named George, entered Celia's life. On several occasions, George "stayed" at Celia's cabin, although whether for a few hours or an entire night is unknown. In late winter, either February or early March, of 1855, Celia again became pregnant. The pregnancy affected George, and caused him to insist that Celia put an end to the pattern of sexual exploitation by Newsom that continued to that time. George informed Celia that "he would have nothing more to do with her if she did not quit the old man" [trial testimony of Jefferson Jones].

Celia approached Newsom's daughters, Virginia and Mary, asking their help in getting Newsom "to quit forcing her while she was sick." It is not clear whether either of the Newsom daughters made any attempt to intervene on Celia's behalf, but it is known that the sexual assaults continued. In desperation, Celia begged Newsom to leave her alone, at least through her pregnancy, but the slave owner was unreceptive to her pleas.

On June 23, 1855, Newsom told Celia "he was coming to her cabin that night." Around 10 P.M., Newsom left his bedroom and walked the fifty yards to Celia's brick cabin. When Newsom told Celia it was time for sex, she retreated to a corner of the cabin. He advanced toward her. Celia then grabbed a stick placed there earlier in the day. Celia raised the stick, "about as large as the upper part of a Windsor chair, but not so long," and struck her master hard over the head. Newsom groaned and "sunk down on a stool or towards the floor." Celia clubbed Newsom over the head a second time, killing him [testimony of Jefferson Jones].

After making sure "he was dead," Celia spent an hour or so pondering her next step. Finally she decided to burn Newsom's body in her fireplace. She went outside to gather staves and used them to build a raging fire. Then she dragged the corpse over to the fireplace and pushed it into the flames. She kept the fire going through the night. In the early morning, she gathered up bone fragments from the ashes and smashed them against the hearth stones, then threw the particles back into the fireplace. A few larger pieces of bone she put "under the hearth, and under the floor between a sleeper and the fireplace." Shortly before daybreak, Celia carried some of the ashes out into the yard and then went to bed.

In the morning, as Newsom's family was growing concerned about Robert's disappearance, Celia enlisted the help of Newsom's grandson, Coffee Waynescot, in shoveling ashes out of her fireplace and into a bucket. Coffee testified later he decided to help when the slave said "she would give me two dozen walnuts if I would carry the ashes out; I said good lick." Following Celia's instruction, Coffee distributed the remains of his grandfather along a path leading to the stables.

Investigation and Inquest

On the morning of the 24th, Virginia Newsom searched for her father in along nearby creek banks and coves, fearing he might have drowned. By mid-morning, the search party grew to include several neighbors and Newsom's son, Harry. After fruitless hours of searching, suspicion began to turn to George, who--it was thought--might have been motivated to kill Newsom out of jealousy. William Powell, owner both of slaves and an adjoining 160-acre farm, questioned George. George denied any knowledge of what might have happened to Newsom, but then added--suspiciously--"it was not worth while to hunt for him any where except close to the house." Faced with, most likely, severe threats, George eventually provided an additional damning bit of information. He told Powell "he believed the last walking [Newsom] had done was along the path, pointing to the path leading from the house to the Negro cabin." George's comment immediately led investigators to the conclusion that Newsom had been killed in Celia's cabin.

When a search of Celia's cabin failed to turn up Newsom's body, Powell and the others located Celia doing her regular duties in the kitchen of the Newsom home. Powell falsely claimed that George had told the search party that "she knew where her master was," hoping this approach might prompt a quick confession from Celia. Instead, Celia denied any knowledge of her master's fate. Faced with escalating threats, including the threat of having her children taken away from her, Celia continued to insist on her innocence. (She undoubtedly understood that confessing to the murder of her master would be an even more serious threat to her relationship with her children.) Eventually, however, Celia admitted that Newsom had indeed visited her cabin seeking sex the previous night. She insisted that Newsom never entered her cabin, but rather that she struck him as he leaned inside the window and "he fell back outside and she saw nothing more of him." Finally, after refusing "for some time to tell anything more," Celia promised to tell more if Powell would "send two men [Newsom's two sons] out of the room." When Harry and David left, Celia confessed to the murder of Robert Newsom.

Following Celia's confession, the search party located Newsom's ashes along the path to the stables. They also gathered bits of bones from Celia's fireplace, larger bone fragments from under the hearth stone, and Newsom's burnt buckle, buttons, and blackened pocketknife. The collected items were placed in a box for display during the inquest that was to come.

Acting on an affidavit filed by David Newsom, the case of State of Missouri v Celia, a Slave commenced. Two justices of the peace, six local residents comprising an inquest jury, and three summoned witnesses all assembled at the Newsom residence on the morning of June 25. William Powell testified first, providing the jurors with an account of his interrogation of Celia the day before. Twelve-year-old Coffee Waynescot told jurors of Celia's request that he distribute what turned out to be his grandfather's ashes along the path. The third and last witness was Celia, who reaffirmed that she killed Newsom, but insisted that "she did not intend to kill him when she struck him, but only wanted to hurt him." The inquest jury quickly determined that probable cause existed that Celia feloniously and willfully murdered Robert

Newsom, and the slave girl was ordered taken to the Callaway County jail in Fulton, nine miles to the north of the Newsom farm.

Doubts as to whether Celia could have pulled off her crime without help lingered, and Callaway County Sheriff William Snell allowed two men, Jefferson Jones and Thomas Shoatman, to conduct further questioning of Celia in her jail cell. Celia added some additional detail to her original story, describing the history of rape and sexual exploitation that began soon after her arrival on the Newsom farm, but she continued to deny that George played any role in Newsom's death or the disposal of his body.

The Trial of Celia

Celia's trial came at a time of heightened tensions over the issue of slavery. In 1854, Congress had passed the Kansas-Nebraska Act, which repealed the Missouri Compromise of 1820 and allowed settlers in those territories to decide for themselves whether to permit slavery within their boundaries. Northern opposition to the new law led to the establishment of the Republican Party and to campaigns by both pro-slavery and anti-slavery groups to influence the outcomes of elections in Kansas. Some prominent Missouri figures, such as

U. S. Senator David Atchinson and University of Missouri President James Shannon, encouraged their slave-state residents to counter the efforts of abolitionists who were moving to Kansas in the hope of keeping it slave-free. Proslavery mobs of Missourians attacked both Free-Soil voters in Kansans and threatened fellow Missourians who dared to criticize their bullying tactics. By the summer of 1855, Missouri was awash with proslavery rhetoric and increasingly active vigilante groups organized to ensure Kansas would enter the Union as a slave state. On October 6, three days before the start of Celia's trial, John Brown arrived in a Kansas that contained two state legislatures, one supporting Kansas's admission as a free state and one enacting slave laws. On Missouri's western border, the possibility of civil war seemed real.

The political implications of Celia's trial could not have escaped Circuit Court Judge William Hall. Certainly, he knew, proslavery Missourians expected Celia to hang. Hall's choice as Celia's defense attorney, John Jameson, was a safe one. Jameson's reputation as a competent, genial member of the bar and his lack of involvement in the heated slavery debates (despite being a slave owner himself) ensured that his selection would not be seriously contested. Jameson could provide the defendant with satisfactory--but not too satisfactory--representation. In addition, Hall appointed two young lawyers, Isaac Boulware and Nathan Kouns, to assist Jameson in his defense.

Celia's jurors, of course, were all male. They ranged in age from thirty-four to seventy-five and, with one exception, were married with children. All were farmers. Several were slave owners.

The prosecution's first witness, Jefferson Jones, described his conversation with Celia in the Callaway County jail. He told jurors Celia's account of the murder and how she had disposed of the body. On cross-examination, Jameson questioned Jones about what Celia had said about the sexual nature of her relationship to the deceased. Jones testified that he had "heard" Newsom raped her soon after her purchase from an Audrain County farmer--and that Celia told him that Newsom had continued to demand sex in the five years that followed. Jones also acknowledged that Celia had told him that she "did not intend to kill" Newsom, "only to hurt him."

Virginia Waynescot, Newsom's eldest daughter, testified next. She described the search for her father on direct examination, testifying, "I hunted on all of the paths and walks and every place for him," including "caves and along the creeks," but "I found no trace of him." Virginia faced questioning on cross-examination concerning Celia's possible motive for the killing. She admitted that Celia became pregnant ("took sick") in February "and had been sick ever since"-- too sick even to cook for the Newsom.

After Coffee Waynescot described for jurors his unknowing dumping of his grandfather's ashes, William Powell took the stand. Jameson cross-examined Powell vigorously, gaining admissions from the search party leader that he had threatened Celia with the loss of her children and with hanging to obtain her confession. Powell also testified that Celia had complained that Newsom repeatedly demanded sex and that the slave girl had approached other Newsom family members in a vain attempt to stop the rapes. Powell also admitted that Celia told him that her attack on Newsom came from desperation and that she only intended to injure, not kill, her master. After Powell's testimony, the prosecution called two doctors who identified the bone fragments found in Celia's cabin as those from an adult human. Following the doctors' testimony, the state rested its case.

Dr. James Martin, a Fulton physician, testified first for the defense. (Celia, as a slave, was not called as a witness. Under the existing law in Missouri and most other states, a criminal defendant could not--under "the interested party rule"--testify.) Jameson posed for Martin questions designed to suggest that Celia was incapable of committing the alleged crime without the aid of another person. The defense attorney asked whether a human body could be so completely destroyed in a simple fireplace in a span of only six or so hours, but the question met with a prosecution objection, which Judge Hall sustained. Jameson tried rephrasing the question a couple of different ways (e.g., "What, in your opinion as a scientific physician, would be the time required to destroy an adult human body?"), but fared no better with the objections and was forced to abandon that line of questioning.

The second and last defense witness, Thomas Shoatman, testified that, during her jail house interview, Celia had said that after she struck Newsom the first time he "he threw his hand up to catch her." The judge, however, again sustained a prosecution objection to the testimony, and jurors were instructed to ignore the evidence that suggested the second and fatal blow came only after Celia was physically threatened. Satisfied, perhaps, that the jury had at least heard the reasons for Celia's desperate act, Jameson rested his case.

Judge Hall's jury instructions made an acquittal all but impossible. He rejected all nine proposed defense instructions that addressed the question of motive or degree of culpability. Among those thrown out were instructions that would have allowed the jury to return a "not guilty" verdict if the jury believed that Celia killed Newsom in an attempt to fight off his sexual advances. The defense, for example, proposed that the jury be told that they could acquit Celia on a self-defense theory if she believed she was "in imminent danger of forced sexual intercourse." Instead of suggesting any viable self-defense argument, Hall instructed jurors that "the defendant had no right to kill [Newsom] because he came into her cabin and was talking to her about having intercourse with her or anything else." Given the threat the defense's proposed instructions presented to established understandings concerning the very minimal rights of slaves, Hall's pro-prosecution instructions should have come as no surprise. Neither, it is likely, was anyone in the Callaway County courthouse surprised when, on October 10, the jury quickly convicted Celia of first-degree murder.

Celia's attorneys appeared again in court the next day to move for a new trial, based on Judge Hall's evidentiary rulings during the proceeding and his allegedly erroneous instructions. Judge Hall took twenty-four hours to consider the defense motion, then rejected it and sentenced Celia to be "hanged by the neck until dead on the sixteenth day of November 1855." The defense motion that it be allowed to appeal the judge's ruling to the Missouri Supreme Court was granted.

Epilogue

In jail awaiting her execution, Celia delivered a stillborn child. As the date for her execution approached, still no word had come from Jefferson City on her appeal filed in the Missouri Supreme Court. The possibility that she might be hanged before her appeal was decided seemed ever more real to Celia's defense team and whoever else she might count among her supporters. Something had to be done.

On November 11, five days before her scheduled date with the gallows, Celia and another inmate were removed from the Callaway County jail, either with the assistance or the knowledge of her defense lawyers. The defense team, in a letter to Supreme Court Justice Abiel Leonard written less than a month after her escape, noted that Celia "was taken out [of jail] by someone" and that they felt "more than ordinary interest in behalf of the girl Celia" owing to the circumstances of her act. Celia was returned to jail--by whom it is not known--in late November, only after her scheduled execution date had passed. Following her return, Judge Hall set a new execution date of December 21--a date, the defense hoped, that would give the Supreme Court time to issue its decision on their appeal.

The Supreme Court ruled against Celia in her appeal. In their December 14 order, the state justices said they "thought it proper to refuse the prayer of the petitioner," having found "no probable cause for her appeal." The stay of execution, the justices wrote, is "refused."

Celia was interviewed for a final time in her cell on the evening before her execution. Again, she denied that "anyone assisted her...or abetted her in any way." She told her interrogator, as reported in the Fulton Telegraph, "as soon as I struck him the Devil got into me, and I struck him with a stick until he was dead, and then rolled him into the fire and burnt him up." Celia died on the gallows at 2:30 P.M. on December 21, 1855.

Source: http://law2.umkc.edu/faculty/projects/ftrials/celia/celiaaccount.html

TRUE STORIES OF THE HORRORS OF SLAVERY

Extract from:

The Capture of a Slaver

by

J. Taylor Wood

I was then ordered to return to the brig, bring on board her crew, leaving only the cook and steward, and to take charge of the prize as Lieutenant Bukett, our first lieutenant, was not yet wholly recovered from an attack of African fever. The crew of twenty men, when brought on board, consisted of Spaniards, Greeks, Malays, Arabs, white and black, but had not one Anglo-Saxon. They were ironed in pairs and put under guard.

From the time we first got on board we had heard moans, cries, and rumblings coming from below, and as soon as the captain and crew were removed, the hatches had been taken off, when there arose a hot blast as from a charnel house, sickening and overpowering. In the hold were three or four hundred human beings, gasping, struggling for breath, dying; their bodies, limbs, faces, all expressing terrible suffering. In their agonizing fight for life, some had torn or wounded themselves or their neighbors dreadfully; some were stiffened in the most unnatural positions. As soon as I knew the condition of things I sent the boat back for the doctor and some whiskey. It returned bringing Captain Thompson, and for an hour or more we were all hard at work lifting and helping the poor creatures on deck, where they were laid out in rows. A little water and stimulant revived most of them; some, however, were dead or too far gone to be resuscitated. The doctor worked earnestly over each one, but seventeen were beyond human skill. As fast as he pronounced them dead they were quickly dropped overboard.

Night closed in with our decks covered so thickly with the ebony bodies that with difficulty we could move about; fortunately they were as quiet as so many snakes. In the meantime the first officer, Mr. Block, was sending up a new topgallant yard, reeving new rigging, repairing the sails, and getting everything ataunto aloft. The Kroomen were busy washing out and fumigating the hold, getting ready for our cargo again. It would have been a very anxious night, except that I felt relieved by the presence of the brig which kept within hail. Soon after daybreak Captain Thompson came on board again, and we made a count of the captives as they were sent below; 188 men and boys, and 166 women and girls. Seeing everything snug and in order the captain returned to the brig, giving me final orders to proceed with all possible dispatch to Monrovia, Liberia, land the negroes, then sail for Porto Praya, Cape de Verde Islands, and report to the commodore. As the brig hauled to the wind and stood to the southward and eastward I dipped my colors, when her crew jumped into the rigging and gave us three cheers, which we returned.

As she drew away from us I began to realize my position and responsibility: a young midshipman, yet in my teens, commanding a prize, with three hundred and fifty prisoners on board, two or three weeks' sail from port, with only a small crew. From the first I kept all hands aft except two men on the lookout, and the weather was so warm that we could all sleep on deck. I also ordered the men never to lay aside their pistols or cutlasses, except when working aloft, but my chief reliance was in my knowledge of the negro,--of his patient, docile disposition. Born and bred a slave he never thought of any other condition, and he accepted the situation without a murmur. I had never heard of blacks rising or attempting to gain their freedom on board a slaver.

TRUE STORIES OF THE HORRORS OF SLAVERY

The Hanging of Amy Spain

View of Darlington Court-House and the sycamore-tree where Amy Spain, the negro slave, was hung by the citizens of Darlington, South Carolina

AMY SPAIN

One of the martyrs of the cause which gave freedom to her race was that of a colored woman named Amy Spain, who was a resident of the town of Darlington, situated in a rich cotton-growing district of South Carolina. At the time a portion of the Union army occupied the town of Darlington she expressed her satisfaction by clasping her hands and exclaiming, "Bless the Lord the Yankees have come!" She could not restrain her emotions. The long night of darkness which had bound her in slavery was about to break away. It was impossible to repress the exuberance of her feelings; and although powerless to aid the advancing deliverers of her caste, or to injure her oppressors, the simple expression of satisfaction at the event sealed her doom. Amy Spain died in the cause of freedom. A section of Sherman's cavalry occupied the town, and without doing any damage passed through. Not an insult nor an unkind word was said to any of the women of that town. The men had, with guilty consciences, fled; but on their return, with their traditional chivalry, they seized upon poor Army, and ignominiously hung her to a sycamore-tree standing in front of the court-house, underneath which stood the block from which was monthly exhibited the slave chattels that were struck down by the auctioneer's hammer to the highest bidder.

Amy Spain heroically heard her sentence, and from her prison bars declared she was prepared to die. She defied her persecutors; and as she ascended the scaffold declared she was going to a place where she would receive a crown of glory. She was rudely interrupted by an oath from one of her executioners. To the eternal disgrace of Darlington her execution was acquiesced in and witnessed by most of the citizens of the town. Amy was launched into eternity, and the "chivalric Southern gentlemen" of Darlington had fully established their bravery by making war upon a defenseless African woman. She sleeps quietly, with others of her race, near the beautiful village. No memorial marks her grave, but after-ages will remember this martyr of liberty. Her persecutors will pass away and be forgotten, but Amy Spain's name is now hallowed among the Africans, who, emancipated and free, dare, with the starry folds of the flag of the free floating over them, speak her name with holy reverence.

From: http://blackhistory.harpweek.com/7Illustrations/Culture/HangingAmySpain.htm

TRUE STORIES OF THE HORRORS OF SLAVERY

The Weeping Time

1859

An American Slave Market

'The blades of grass on all the Butler estates are outnumbered by the tears that are poured out in agony at the wreck that has been wrought in happy homes, and the crushing grief that has been laid on loving hearts.'

—*Mortimer Thomson (Philander Doesticks)*

Irishman Pierce Butler, a Major in the British Army, was born to an aristocratic Irish family on July 11, 1744 in County Carlow, Ireland. As the third son, he could not inherit his father's title or land, so his father purchased a British Army commission for Pierce. In 1767, Major Butler went to South Carolina with the 29th Regiment of Foot, where they were tasked with suppressing colonial resistance to Parliament. While there in 1771, he married heiress Mary Middleton and became a very rich man. Butler sold his commission and purchased large parcels of land in South Carolina. When the Revolutionary War began Pierce Butler owned 10,000 acres on which he operated rice plantations and oversaw a labor force of Negro slaves. When the war began, Butler became an officer in South Carolina's militia and trained locals to fight off invading British soldiers. By the end of the war, Pierce Butler and his wife had lost their land

and fortune. Elected a Senator from South Carolina, Butler wrote the fugitive slave clause in Article 4 of the United States Constitution. That phrase required slaves who escaped to another state be returned to the owner in the state from which they escaped.

Pierce Butler began rebuilding his personal land and property holdings and by 1793 owned 500 slaves that worked on his rice plantation on Butler Island and cotton plantation at St. Simons Island, both part of the Sea Islands of Georgia. Before his death on February 15, 1822, Pierce Butler owned more than 1,000 slaves and 10,000 acres of land. The elder Pierce Butler left nothing to his children and his entire estate only to his grandchildren who would change their last name to Butler.

Major Butler's eldest daughter, Sarah Butler, married James Mease and they had five children, including Pierce Butler Mease on March 23, 1810 in Philadelphia, who changed his name to Pierce Mease Butler to qualify to inherit a share of his maternal grandfather's estate. As his grandfather's namesake, Pierce M. Butler inherited Butler's Plantation on Butler Island, Georgia. Most Americans of their day would never have heard about Butler Island or the slaves the Butler family owned if, in 1834, Pierce M. Butler had not married Frances Anne "Fannie" Kemble, an actress and staunch abolitionist from London, England.

Though constantly assured that the slaves were treated well, never sold and content in their circumstances, in 1838 Fannie wanted to see for herself and spent four months in residence on Butler Island. That visit led to their divorce and her writing a book she titled Journal of a Residence on a Georgia Plantation. She was appalled at the sight of "filthy and wretched" slave dwellings that lacked tables and chairs, knives and forks, and decent bedding. Children were dirty, barefoot and uneducated. While it was true that slaves were not sold, she complained that they were "sold-out" to work on other plantations. She also noticed that the plantation on St. Simons Island had more mulatto slaves than at Butler Island. Pierce explained that white men had easier access to that plantation than at Butler Island. Fannie noticed that one slave looked exactly like Roswell King and his son, Roswell King, Jr. They had managed the Butler family plantations for years under Major Pierce Butler. Slaves on both plantations told Fannie that the Roswells had fathered a number of children with many slaves. Sickened by what she saw and heard, Fannie left the Sea Islands, filed for divorce and returned to England.

The story of Pierce Mease Butler and his slaves continued on for 20 years, culminating when Pierce's financial empire collapsed in 1859 under the weight of enormous debt. Out of options, Butler had to sell his human property to satisfy creditors at what would be the largest sale of slaves on record in the United States. The sale took place on March 2-3, 1850 at the Ten Broeck Race Course in Savannah, Georgia. Buyers purchased 436 men, women and children from his Butler Island and Hampton plantations near Darien, Georgia. Although Butler asked that families be sold together, that wouldn't be the case for many and the event would be remembered as "the weeping time." Newspapers and magazines reported the event nationwide and as the historical marker placed in remembrance of the event says, "and reaction to the sale deepened the nation's growing sectional divide in the years immediately preceding the Civil War." Johni Cerny

Pierce Mease Butler

ADVERTISMENT

FOR SALE. LONG COTTON AND RICE NEGROES.

A Gang of 460 Negroes, accustomed to the culture of Rice and Provisions; among whom are a number of good mechanics, and house servants. Will be sold on the 2d and 3d of March next, at Savannah, by JOSEPH BRYAN. Terms of Sale—One-third cash; remainder by bond, bearing interest from day of sale, payable in two equal annual instalments, to be secured by mortgage on the negroes, and approved personal security, or for approved city acceptance on Savannah or Charleston. Purchasers paying for papers. The Negroes will be sold in families, and can be seen on the premises of JOSEPH BRYAN, In Savannah, three days prior to the day of sale, when catalogues will be furnished. *** The Charleston Courier.

"The premises of JOSEPH BRYAN" referred to Bryan's slave holding and trading pen on Savannah's Johnson Square. Inspection of the enslaved would have begun on February 26, the very day Bryan introduced another, modified ad about the impending slave sale in both The Savannah Republican and The Savannah Daily Morning News. Bryan changed the venue to the "Race Course," and reduced the number of persons for sale:

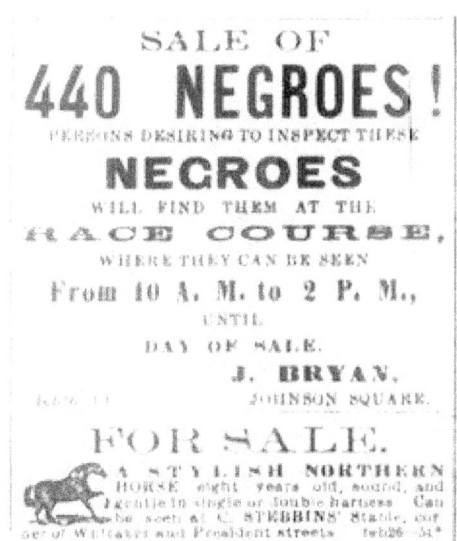

SALE OF 440 NEGROES! PERSONS DESIRING TO INSPECT THESE NEGROES WILL FIND THEM AT THE RACE COURSE, WHERE THEY CAN BE SEEN From 10 A.M. to 2 P.M., UNTIL DAY OF SALE. J. BRYAN. JOHNSON SQUARE.

The event came to be called the **Weeping Time** by the slaves and their descendants, "because of reports that the sky opened up and poured down rain for the full two days of the auction. It was said that the heavens were weeping for the inhumanity that was being committed."

It is a dreadful affair, however, selling these hereditary Negroes. . . . Families will not be separated, that is to say, husbands and wives, parents and young children. But brothers and sisters of mature age, parents and children of mature age, all other relations and the ties of home and long association will be violently severed. It will be a hard thing for Butler to witness and it is a monstrous thing to do. Yet it is done every day in the South. It is one among the many frightful consequences of slavery and contradicts our civilization, our Christianity, or Republicanism. Can such a system endure, is it consistent with humanity, with moral progress? These are difficult questions, and still more difficult is it to say, what can be done? The Negroes of the South must be slaves or the South will be Africanized. Slavery is better for them and for us than such a result.

Mortimer Thomson, a popular newsman of the day known affectionately as "Doesticks," wrote a lengthy, uncomplimentary article about the auction for the New York Tribune entitled "What Became of the Slaves on a Georgia Plantation." He reported how the slaves, eager to impress potential masters who they perceived as kind, would sometimes cheerfully respond to buyers "pulling their mouths open to see their teeth, pinching their limbs to find how muscular they were, walking them up and down to detect any signs of lameness, making them stoop and bend in different ways that they might be certain there was no concealed rupture or wound. . . ." And Thomson commiserated with the unfortunate slaves after the sale, stating, "On the faces of all was an expression of heavy grief; some appeared to be resigned to the hard stroke of Fortune that had torn them from their homes, and were sadly trying to make the best of it; some sat brooding moodily over their sorrows, their chins resting on their hands, their eyes staring vacantly, and their bodies rocking to and fro, with a restless motion that was never stilled. . . ."

After four days of prodding and inspection by prospective buyers, the slaves suffered through the two-day sale. Some stood stoically, resignedly, attempting to keep their dignity, while buyers poked, pinched, and fondled them, looked into their mouths, insisted they bend over or extend their limbs, and searched for 'ruptures' or 'defects' that might affect their future productivity.15 Doesticks described the buyers as "generally of a rough breed, slangy, profane and bearish," including some "fast young men," "rough backwood rowdies" and also "[w]hite neck-clothed, gold-spectacled, and silver-haired old men." Pretend-buyer Doesticks recorded the facts of the sale, and his observations of the emotional impact on the men, women, and children (including thirty babies), who were sold for a sum of $303,850.16

Parents were separated from children, and betrothed from each other. Among the many wrenching stories Doesticks describes is that of a young, enslaved man, Jeffrey, twenty-three years old, who pleaded with his purchaser to also buy Dorcas, his beloved:

"I loves Dorcas, young mas'r; I loves her well an' true; she says she loves me, and I know she does; de good Lord knows I loves her better than I loves any on in de wide world - never can love another woman half so well. Please buy Dorcas, mas'r. We're be good sarvants to you long as we live. We're be married right soon, young mas'r, and de chillum will be healthy and strong, mas'r and dey'll be good sarvants, too. Please buy Dorcas, young mas'r. We loves each other a heap—do, really, true, mas'r."

Realizing that his love alone would not impress his new "mas'r," Jeffrey tried to appeal to his purchaser's business sense by "marketing" his own prospective bride, in a desperate hope that they might be together:

"Young mas'r, Dorcas prime woman—A1 woman, sa. Tall gal, sir; long arms, strong, healthy, and can do a heap of work in a day. She is one of de best rice hands on de whole plantation; worth $1,200 easy, mas'r and fus rate bargain at that."

What is evident is the humanity of Jeffrey, Dorcas, and all the others seemingly commoditized by this sale. Jeffrey makes clear his love for Dorcas, and his plans for a future with her—a family that would include children, if even they would all be enslaved. Given the uncertainty of slavery, with its immanence of impending loss and unpredictable futures, Jeffrey felt that his best odds were to help broker his sweetheart's sale, and to suggest her market value.

Jeffrey's new owner considered purchasing Dorcas until he realized that she was to be sold in a family of four, and could not be purchased independently. When Jeffrey's entreaties came to nothing and Dorcas was bought by someone else, he walked away and grieved, consoled in silence by a circle of his enslaved friends.20 Jeffrey and Dorcas were separated, ironically, because Pierce Butler had required that, to the extent possible, the enslaved be sold in "families."

In "'We'm Fus' Rate Bargain': Value, Labor, and Price in a Georgia Slave Community," Daina Ramey Berry explains that "Because [Jeffrey and Dorcas] were not married, there was no chance that they would be sold as a family." She points to the desperation that leads Jeffrey to suggest a purchase price for his beloved. While planters and agents were purchasing slaves "based on economic interest," the enslaved approached the auction block "with overt manipulation and covert strategies to maintain family ties . . . to try to keep relatives and loved ones together."

Doesticks also tells of Daphne, a young woman who was wrapped in a shawl when ordered to mount the auction block. Buyers, bothered that they were thwarted from making "a thorough examination of her limbs," insisted that Daphne expose herself to their full scrutiny, one asking, "Who is going to bid on that nigger, if you keep her covered up? Let's see her face." Mr. Walsh, the auctioneer, spoke to the two hundred buyers gathered at the platform and let it be known that Daphne had "been confined only fifteen days [earlier]," and that he felt "on that account she was entitled to the slight indulgence of a blanket, to keep from herself and child the chill air and the driving rain."22 A week after Daphne had given birth she, her husband, and their other small child, along with other enslaved, were sent up to Savannah from the Butler plantations. The family sold for $2,500.23

In revealing emotions experienced by the slaves, Doesticks paid particular attention to facial expressions and body language:

On the faces of all was an expression of heavy grief; some appeared to be resigned to the hard stroke of Fortune that had torn them from their homes, and were sadly trying to make the best of it; some sat brooding moodily over their sorrows, their chins resting on their hands, their eyes staring vacantly, and their bodies rocking to and fro, with a restless motion that was never stilled; few wept, the place was too public and the drivers too near, though some occasionally turned aside to give way to a few quiet tears.24

Resignation mixed with dignity and pain to tide the enslaved over during this wrenching transition from one place, and one bondage, to another:

The expression on the faces of all who stepped on the block was always the same, and told of more anguish than it is in the power of words to express. Blighted homes, crushed hopes and broken hearts was the sad story to be read in all the anxious faces. Some of them regarded the sale with perfect indifference, never making a motion save to turn from one side to the other at the word of the dapper Mr. Bryan, that all the crowd might have a fair view of their proportions, and then, when the sale was accomplished, stepped down from the block without caring to cast even a look at the buyer, who now held all their happiness in his hands.25

The "Weeping Time" brought much anguish to the enslaved. Families, who had been together for all of their lives on Butler's Island or Hampton, were torn apart and dispersed; many of them never saw each other again. The Butler slaves were dispersed all over the southern states. The heavens seemed to weep in empathy as the four dry days during which buyers inspected the enslaved gave way to a brooding storm; it rained "violently," and the "wind howled" for the two days of sale, letting up only after the last person had been sold.26 Outside the advertisements, the Savannah newspapers offered cursory mention that the sale had taken place as planned. Slavery and slave sales were a way of life and livelihood in Savannah, and much of the US South. After Mortimer Thomson's Tribune article was published in the North, Savannah Morning News editor, William T. Thompson (1812–1882) castigated Doesticks as a spy, intimating that next time he came South, he would not get away.

Detailing the callousness and heartlessness of slavery, Doesticks' published exposé was a political blow to the South, at a time of escalating sectional animosity. Like the arrival of the slave ship Wanderer—which in November 1858 landed the last shipment of African slaves brought to Georgia, on Jekyll Island near Savannah, the Ten Broeck slave sale exacerbated tensions between northern and southern states.

After the Civil War, some Butler slaves returned to the plantations where they had been born or raised, where they felt most connected, in search of friends and families. Descendants of Butler slaves still live in Darien, Brunswick, St. Simons Island, and vicinity. Other Butler descendants can be found in Savannah, Charleston, Memphis and New Orleans, where the Butler slave sale was advertised, and in smaller nearby towns. Narratives of the "Weeping Time" have persisted among some African Americans of the Georgia Low Country.29 The efforts of Monifa Johnson, a contemporary resident of Savannah who was aware of this history, led to her city's commemorating the site.

The two-day sale netted $303,850. The highest price paid for one family -- a mother and her five grown children -- was $6,180. The highest price for one individual was $1,750. The lowest price for any one slave was $250.

Soon after the last slave was sold, the rain stopped. Champagne bottles popped in celebration. And Pierce Butler, once again wealthy, made a trip to southern Europe before returning home to Philadelphia.

TRUE STORIES OF THE HORRORS OF SLAVERY

Specimens of Advertisements in Public Papers

CHARLES DICKENS

From His Publication: American Notes for General Circulation approx. 1842

The following are a few specimens of the advertisements in the public papers. It is only four years since the oldest among them appeared; and others of the same nature continue to be published every day, in shoals.

'Ran away, Negress Caroline. Had on a collar with one prong turned down.'

'Ran away, a black woman, Betsy. Had an iron bar on her right leg.'

'Ran away, the negro Manuel. Much marked with irons.'

'Ran away, the negress Fanny. Had on an iron band about her neck.'

'Ran away, a negro boy about twelve years old. Had round his neck a chain dog-collar with "De Lampert" engraved on it.'

'Ran away, the negro Hown. Has a ring of iron on his left foot. Also, Grise, his wife, having a ring and chain on the left leg.'

'Ran away, a negro boy named James. Said boy was ironed when he left me.'

'Committed to jail, a man who calls his name John. He has a clog of iron on his right foot which will weigh four or five pounds.'

'Detained at the police jail, the negro wench, Myra. Has several marks of lashing, and has irons on her feet.'

'Ran away, a negro woman and two children. A few days before she went off, I burnt her with a hot iron, on the left side of her face. I tried to make the letter M.'

'Ran away, a negro man named Henry; his left eye out, some scars from a dirk on and under his left arm, and much scarred with the whip.'

'One hundred dollars reward, for a negro fellow, Pompey, 40 years old. He is branded on the left jaw.'

'Committed to jail, a negro man. Has no toes on the left foot.'

'Ran away, a negro woman named Rachel. Has lost all her toes except the large one.'

'Ran away, Sam. He was shot a short time since through the hand, and has several shots in his left arm and side.'

'Ran away, my negro man Dennis. Said negro has been shot in the left arm between the shoulder and elbow, which has paralysed the left hand.'

'Ran away, my negro man named Simon. He has been shot badly, in his back and right arm.'

'Ran away, a negro named Arthur. Has a considerable scar across his breast and each arm, made by a knife; loves to talk much of the goodness of God.'

'Twenty-five dollars reward for my man Isaac. He has a scar on his forehead, caused by a blow; and one on his back, made by a shot from a pistol.'

'Ran away, a negro girl called Mary. Has a small scar over her eye, a good many teeth missing, the letter A is branded on her cheek and forehead.'

'Ran away, negro Ben. Has a scar on his right hand; his thumb and forefinger being injured by being shot last fall. A part of the bone came out. He has also one or two large scars on his back and hips.'

'Detained at the jail, a mulatto, named Tom. Has a scar on the right cheek, and appears to have been burned with powder on the face.'

'Ran away, a negro man named Ned. Three of his fingers are drawn into the palm of his hand by a cut. Has a scar on the back of his neck, nearly half round, done by a knife.'

'Was committed to jail, a negro man. Says his name is Josiah. His back very much scarred by the whip; and branded on the thigh and hips in three or four places, thus (J M). The rim of his right ear has been bit or cut off.'

'Fifty dollars reward, for my fellow Edward. He has a scar on the corner of his mouth, two cuts on and under his arm, and the letter E on his arm.'

'Ran away, negro boy Ellie. Has a scar on one of his arms from the bite of a dog.'

'Ran away, from the plantation of James Surgette, the following negroes: Randal, has one ear cropped; Bob, has lost one eye; Kentucky Tom, has one jaw broken.'

'Ran away, Anthony. One of his ears cut off, and his left hand cut with an axe.'

'Fifty dollars reward for the negro Jim Blake. Has a piece cut out of each ear, and the middle finger of the left hand cut off to the second joint.'

'Ran away, a negro woman named Maria. Has a scar on one side of her cheek, by a cut. Some scars on her back.'

'Ran away, the Mulatto wench Mary. Has a cut on the left arm, a scar on the left shoulder, and two upper teeth missing.'

I should say, perhaps, in explanation of this latter piece of description, that among the other blessings which public opinion secures to the negroes, is the common practice of violently punching out their teeth. To make them wear iron collars by day and night, and to worry them with dogs, are practices almost too ordinary to deserve mention.

'Ran away, my man Fountain. Has holes in his ears, a scar on the right side of his forehead, has been shot in the hind part of his legs, and is marked on the back with the whip.'

'Two hundred and fifty dollars reward for my negro man Jim. He is much marked with shot in his right thigh. The shot entered on the outside, halfway between the hip and knee joints.'

'Brought to jail, John. Left ear cropt.'

'Taken up, a negro man. Is very much scarred about the face and body, and has the left ear bit off.'

'Ran away, a black girl, named Mary. Has a scar on her cheek, and the end of one of her toes cut off.'

'Ran away, my Mulatto woman, Judy. She has had her right arm broke.'

'Ran away, my negro man, Levi. His left hand has been burnt, and I think the end of his forefinger is off.'

'Ran away, a negro man, named Washington. Has lost a part of his middle finger, and the end of his little finger.'

'Twenty-five dollars reward for my man John. The tip of his nose is bit off.'

'Twenty-five dollars reward for the negro slave, Sally. Walks as though crippled in the back.'

'Ran away, Joe Dennis. Has a small notch in one of his ears.'

'Ran away, negro boy, Jack. Has a small crop out of his left ear.'

'Ran away, a negro man, named Ivory. Has a small piece cut out of the top of each ear.'

While upon the subject of ears, I may observe that a distinguished abolitionist in New York once received a negro's ear, which had been cut off close to the head, in a general post letter. It was forwarded by the free and independent gentleman who had caused it to be amputated, with a polite request that he would place the specimen in his 'collection.'

I could enlarge this catalogue with broken arms, and broken legs, and gashed flesh, and missing teeth, and lacerated backs, and bites of dogs, and brands of red-hot irons innumerable: but as my readers will be sufficiently sickened and repelled already, I will turn to another branch of the subject.

These advertisements, of which a similar collection might be made for every year, and month, and week, and day; and which are coolly read in families as things of course, and as a part of the current news and small-talk; will serve to show how very much the slaves profit by public opinion, and how tender it is in their behalf. But it may be worth while to inquire how the slave-owners, and the class of society to which great numbers of them belong, defer to public opinion in their conduct, not to their slaves but to each other; how they are accustomed to restrain their passions; what their bearing is among themselves; whether they are fierce or gentle; whether their social customs be brutal, sanguinary, and violent, or bear the impress of civilisation and refinement.

That we may have no partial evidence from abolitionists in this inquiry, either, I will once more turn to their own newspapers, and I will confine myself, this time, to a selection from paragraphs which appeared from day to day, during my visit to America, and which refer to occurrences happening while I was there. The italics in these extracts, as in the foregoing, are my own.

These cases did not all occur, it will be seen, in territory actually belonging to legalised Slave States, though most, and those the very worst among them did, as their counterparts constantly do; but the position of the scenes of action in reference to places immediately at hand, where slavery is the law; and the strong resemblance between that class of outrages and the rest; lead to the just presumption that the character of the parties concerned was formed in slave districts, and brutalised by slave customs.

TRUE STORIES OF THE HORRORS OF SLAVERY

RECOLLECTIONS OF SLAVERY

by

A Runaway Slave

The Emancipator, August 23, September 13, September 20, October 11, October 18, 1838

'I have heard a great deal said about hell, and wicked places, but I don't think there is any worse hell than that sugar house.'

I ran away from Cohen because he whipped me. A black man stole some hog meat and hid it for his wife under his house. The overseer, in searching about after stolen things, found it, and then whipped me to make me tell who put it there, because they thought I knew. As soon as they had done, master sent me to get the mules, but I kept right on into the swamp; I never came back. I went off to Four Holes and staid some days in the woods round Bradwell's plantation, where my sister lived, before I could get a chance to speak to her. At last I hid near the field where she was hoeing and got close to her row, and when she came along I contrived to let her know I was there. After a while we got a chance to talk together, and she told me that Cohen had offered 50 dollars for me, and said she wished I would get some of the hands to ask Bradwell to buy me. She thought he would be willing to. I staid about there nearly a month, talking with the people every night. One drizzly night when I was in the mule lot among the slaves, a man named John Strutts dodged round the corner of the fence, and hid behind the mules, so that I could not see him, and then he called to me and told me to stand still till he tied me.

After he tied me he took me to his house and kept me till next morning, and then carried me to the Sugar House in Charleston. As soon as we got there they made me strip off all my clothes, and searched me to see if I had anything hid. They found nothing but a knife. After that they drove me into the yard where I staid till night. As soon as master's father, Mordecai Cohen, heard that I was caught, he sent word to his son, and the next morning master came. He said "well, you staid in the woods as long as you could, now which will you do,--stay here, or go home?" I told him I did'nt know. Then he said if I would not go home willingly I might stay there two or three months. He said "Mr. Wolf, give this fellow fifty lashes and put him on the tread mill. I'm going North, and shall not be back till July, and you may keep him till that time." He said this just to make me say I would go back with him, for he had no intention of going to the

North. As soon as Cohen turned his back, Wolf whistled, and two drivers came, and he told them to put me in the rope.

When they had got me fixed in the rope good, and the cap on my face, they called Mr. Jim Wolf, and told him they had me ready. He came and stood till they had done whipping me. One drew me up tight by the rope and the other whipped, and Wolf felt of my skin to tell when it was tight enough. They whipped till he stamped. Then they rubbed brine in, and put on my old clothes which were torn into rags while I was in the swamp, and put me into a cell. The cells are little narrow rooms about five feet wide, with a little hole up high to let in air.

I was kept in the cell till next day, when they put me on the tread mill, and kept me there three days, and then back in the cell for three days. And then I was whipped and put on the tread mill again, and they did so with me for a fortnight, just as Cohen had directed. He told them to whip me twice a week till they had given me two hundred lashes. My back, when they went to whip me, would be full of scabs, and they whipped them off till I bled so that my clothes were all wet. Many a night I have laid up there in the Sugar House and scratched them off by the handful.

In a few more weeks master came and asked if I was ready to go home now. I told him I "did'nt know." The truth was, the sugar house was worse than the plantation, but I would not tell him so. When he found I was stubborn, and would be likely to run away again if he took me out, he said he would keep me there till the speculators came along in the fall. Pretty soon I grew sickly, and when he say how poor I was, and thought I should not live till fall, he set me up to vendue. They bid 670 dollars for me, but he would not sell me for that. He said he would have his price, or I should stay in the sugar house till I died. Afterwards a good many came to see me. They felt of me and said I was thin. Master kept me there a few days longer, and then sold me to John Fogle for 700 dollars. I cost him twelve hundred. It was in June, 1837, when he sold me.

I have heard a great deal said about hell, and wicked places, but I don't think there is any worse hell than that sugar house. It's as bad a place as can be. In getting to it you have to go through a gate, in a very high brick wall. On the top of the wall, both sides of the gate, there are sharp pointed iron bars sticking up, and all along the rest of the wall are broken glass bottles. These are to keep us from climbing over. After you get into the yard, you go through a gate into the entry, then through a door of wood and an iron door, chained and locked together, so as both to open at the same time. The lower story is built of stone of great thickness,--and above, brick. The building is ceiled inside with plank. Away down in the ground, under the house is a dungeon, very cold and so dark you can't tell the difference between day and night. There are six or seven long rooms, and six little cells above and six below. The room to do the whipping in is by itself. When you get in there, every way you look you can see paddles, and whips, and cowskins, and bluejays, and cat-o'-nine tails. The bluejay has two lashes, very heavy and full of knots. It is the worst thing to whip with of any thing they have. It makes a hole where it strikes, and when they have done it will be all bloody.

In the middle of the floor are two big sills, with rings in them, fastened to staples. There are ropes tied to the rings to bind your feet. Over the sills is a windlass, with a rope coming down to fasten your hands to. This rope leads off to the corner of the room, and there are pegs there to tie it to, after they have got you stretched.

Slaves are carried there to be whipped by the people in the country four or five miles round, and by all the people in the city, and the guard men carry there all the runaways they take up. Some would want their niggers whipped with the cowskin and paddled on top of that, and some with the paddle alone, because the paddle blisters and peels the skin all up. They wet the paddle, and then rub it in sand, and every time they hit with it, the skin peels off just the same as you peel a potato. When it gets well it will be right smooth, and not in knots as when whipped with the cowskin. Some would want their niggers whipped with one thing and some with another, and some would'nt care how they were whipped, so they got it.

Mr. Wesley or Wesler was the keeper while I was there, and Mr. Wolf was the clerk. As soon as a slave was brought to be whipped, Mr. Wolf whistled, and two drivers came. If it was a man, they fixed him in the rope themselves, but if a woman they called a woman to do it. When she had got her fixed she let them know, and they went in to whip her. Both men and women were stripped entirely naked, except a small piece of cloth round the body, and a cap was drawn over their face. Mr. Wolf always went in to see that they were stretched tight enough, and to count the lashes. As soon as they had given enough he stamped. You may hear the whip and paddle there, all hours in the day. There's no stopping. As soon as one is loosed from the rope, another is ready to be put in. Some days they have so many brought to be punished that they don't get through till late at night. It's just the same on Sunday as any other day--there's no difference. It's going on all day long. Some people carry their slaves there themselves, and some send them with a letter to the clerk. As soon as he reads it, he whistles for the drivers, and has them tied in the rope. The clerk is a mighty bad man; he never cared what he did with any of us. One morning he beat one of the women over the head with the shovel, because she did not do her sewing.

Mrs. Wolf keeps the women at work, sewing for her all the time, and she used to tell Mr. Wolf that he ought to give them one or two cuts more than the law says, to make them work better.

Widow women, every week, brought their slaves to be whipped. Some went away and left them, and some went into the whipping room and stayed till it was over. They would say, 'how does that feel? Which had you rather do, have that, or mind your business?' A young woman once came and brought three to whip and one to sell. Elizabeth, about 17 or 18 years old, was one brought to whip. She was an Indian girl, with straight black hair. She was a seamstress, and dressed in pretty good clothes. Sancho laid on as hard as he could. She screamed and hallowed in the rope, and Wolf said, 'Can't you stop that woman's mouth, Sancho?'--then he pulled the cap close down to her chin. Sancho was the best driver they had, because he could whip better. He whipped slow, and waited after striking till they turned round, and then struck again.

TRUE STORIES OF THE HORRORS OF SLAVERY

AN EPIC LOVE STORY

By

James A. Haught

Volume 32, Number 2 (January 1971), pp. 101-107

A rich plantation owner chose one of his slaves for his lifelong mate, had thirteen children by her, and finally was killed by angry white neighbors - but not before he took elaborate legal steps to guarantee that his black woman and brown children would inherit all his money and land.

They did, and the former slave plantation eventually turned into the academic community of Institute.

Strangely, the story isn't recorded in any West Virginia history book, even though it was a minor sensation at the end of the Civil War.

Skimpy bits of the tale can be found in century-old handwritten records filed away in the chambers of the Kanawha County clerk and circuit clerk.

The central figure was Samuel I. Cabell, a wealthy pioneer with a strong will and a strong temper. One record in the courthouse says he was born in Georgia; some descendants say family stories indicate he was born in England.

Wherever he came from, there's little doubt he was part of the powerful Cabell family of Virginia that produced generals, Congressmen, a governor and countless judges and bankers. Cabell County is named for the Virginia governor of that name.

One hearsay family account says Samuel I. Cabell acquired many slaves in tideland Virginia, crossed over the mountains to the Kanawha Valley, and worked his slaves for a while in the pioneer salt operations here.

One of his slaves was Mary Barnes, apparently a young black woman, of some physical charm. In the manner of many slaveholders, Cabell took her for his own and began fathering mulatto children.

But unlike other slaveowners, he didn't merely use her as one slave bedmate among many, and then ignore both her and the children that resulted. Instead, he evidently became devoted to her, remained loyal to her all his life, accepted her children proudly, and went to great lengths to guarantee that they had full legal rights as his sons and daughters.

He wrote four different wills to protect his dark-skinned family, and also filed papers setting each member free from slavery. All five documents remain today in aged yellow books at the courthouse, written in the ornate script of a court scrivener.

The earliest will is dated November 24,1851. It says Cabell had no real estate at that time, so he apparently was living somewhere in Kanawha County and using his slaves in industrial work.

The will provided that all his slaves were to be hired out for work for six years after his death, then set free. All, that is, except one select group -

. . . My woman, Mary Barnes, together with all her children. . . I do hereby give their freedom to take effect immediately at my death, and they aren't to be considered as included among the slaves before-mentioned. . . .

He ordered all his personal wealth, and all the money earned by hiring out his other slaves, to be divided among Mary and her children.

The next record in the courthouse is a property deed dated April 8, 1853, showing that Cabell paid $10,500 for 967 acres of rich Kanawha River bottomland encompassing everything between what is now West Dunbar and Sattes. (It was part of a tract once granted to George Washington by the king of England, then regranted to Washington by the governor of Virginia after the Revolution, then left to Martha Washington after George's death, and finally divided among various inheritors.)

Cabell moved his Negro mate and children and his slaves to his new land and began a plantation.

The next record is the partiarch's [sic] second will, dated April 6, 1858. It seems to imply he was worried he might be killed, and that Mary and the children might be sold into slavery if he were. The will begins:

In the event of sudden demise, this instrument of writing is intended to show or make known that Mary Barnes and all her children - namely, Elizabeth, Sam, Lucy, Mary Jane, Sidney Ann, Soula, Eunice, Alice, Marina (or Bobby), Braxton, and an infant not named - are and always have been free, as I have every right to believe they are my children.

I want and it is my will that they shall be educated out of. . . all the moneys, bonds, debts due me, land, stocks, farming utensils and household to be equally divided between them. . . .

Five months later, in a county deed book (slaves were property, remember) it is recorded that Cabell officially set free Mary and the eleven children. The infant had been named Betty by then. (Two more sons, William Clifford and James B., eventually were born.)

Next, still another will was written May 9, 1859. In it Cabell repeated his earlier wishes and spelled out individual cash awards ranging from $2,000 to $3,500 which he wanted bestowed on each child. Some of the daughters had married by this time.

Finally, on September 12, 1863 - during the Civil War - the plantation owner wrote an angry codicil which said:

I hereby revoke this testament and will as to the slave portion. Those that have absconded and those taken away by the Federal Army shall not receive anything and they shall never be released from bondage during their lives. All property and moneys and debts due me shall be given to Mary Barnes and children equally after paying the board and schooling of the six youngest until they arrive of age.

The old man's temper, or his unusual marital status, or something, apparently drew him into conflict with white residents of the valley. In the aged records of Kanawha County Circuit Court, it's written that Cabell was indicted April 5, 1864, on a charge of "intimidating a public officer." But he was released upon pledging to be peaceable thereafter.

The next county record is a single line in a death book:

(Name) Samuel I. Cabell, (date of death) July 18, 1865, (location) Kanawha River, (cause) murdered, (age) about 60, (parents) -. (place of birth Georgia, (consort) - (occupation) farmer. . . .

A weekly Charleston newspaper of that day, the West Virginia Journal, was a fiery abolitionist sheet that regularly devoted its front page to poetry, sermons and demands for the hanging of all "rebel conspirators" such as "the archtraitor, Robert E. Lee." On page 3 of its July 26, 1865 issue (as recorded on microfilm in the State Department of Archives and History), it reported:

The Killing of Samuel I. Cabell

The community here was thrown into considerable excitement on last Thursday evening, by the report of the death of Samuel I. Cabell, a bitter and open rebel who lived some nine miles below Charleston.

Seven have been arrested. Their names are Allen Spradling, Andrew Jackson Spradling, Mark L. Spradling, Stark B. Whittington, Lawrence Whittington, William Whittington and Christopher Williams.

The rumors of the causes leading to this crime are so contradictory that it is impossible to give any reliable statement of the facts; but if, as the friends of the deceased maintain, the act was a premeditated murder, the guilty party should be punished to the full extent of the law. We have already held up the law as the true guide, and nothing can justify its violation.

On the other hand, it is held by friends of the prisoners that they had been subjects of repeated insults on account of their loyalty to the Union, and that they went to his house for the purpose of telling him they would put up with them no longer, when, getting excited, Cabell jumped over the fence flourishing his knife, and he was shot in self-defense.

We can express no opinion, however, until the evidence is revealed.

Unfortunately, the evidence never is revealed - not in any remaining public record. In its next issue, the West Virginia Journal gives no facts, only polemics:

.. .It was established, we believe, that it wasn't a premedidated murder. The charge that the "Union League" is responsible for Cabell's death contains about as much truth as that the Union men of this country are "blood-thirsty", etc. The society spoken of is distinctly a UNION society. Its purposes are LAWFUL and its members LAW-ABIDING.

Later editions merely report that all seven defendants were acquitted, by juries that deliberated only a few minutes in each case. Official records in the circuit clerk's office report simply that the accused men were found innocent.

Folklore around Institute says Cabell was killed because of white resentment toward his integrated family life. But there's no record to confirm it.

It's possible that the white community may not even have been aware of Cabell's personal life - he may have appeared to be only a bachelor farmer living with his slave workers - because the wills which claim Mary and the children weren't brought to the courthouse and filed until after his death.

In December, 1865, Kanawha County commissioners ruled that the wills were valid. (Folklore says white relatives of Cabell tried to break the wills, but no court record shows it. There's no mention of it in circuit court or State Supreme Court records, and the county commissioner records for that period are missing.)

At this point, another rich, white Cabell enters the records. Charleston banker-farmer-salt manufacturer Napoleon Bonaparte Cabell, founder of an influential Kanawha Valley family, was named legal guardian for the youngest six of Samuel I. Cabell's mulatto children. Descendants say Napoleon was either Samuel's brother or his cousin - exact family records have been lost. Neither man is listed in the famous family's genealogy, a thick volume titled The Cabells and their Kin.

(Napoleon Cabell apparently was as fiery as Samuel. Napoleon died in 1889, and his will in the county records is a ferocious one. He disinherited two daughters who married against his wishes, calling one of the sons-in-law "no better than a thief. . .He swindled me out of about

$2000." As for his wife. Napoleon recorded that "she never brought a farthing along" when he married her.)

Other county records tell the rest of the story.

In 1869, Mary Barnes petitioned the county commissioners to change her and her children's name to Cabell. In 1870, the commissioners divided the Cabell land among the mother and children, giving each a strip from the river to the hill. In 1871, executors reported that the Cabell estate was worth $42,128 - a considerable fortune a century ago, equivalent to at least a half-million dollars today.

Before he was killed, Samuel Cabell had striven to give his children the best possible education. There were no schools for Negroes in West Virginia, so he sent them to a private academy in Ohio. The practice continued after his death, and the youngsters grew to be an 1870s rarity; educated, professional-class Negroes. Some were doctors, some became teachers.

Some of the children settled in other states. Some returned to the family homestead in Kanawha County. Those who remained here became leaders among the growing number of residents as the plantation gradually evolved into a town.

The community was called, at different times, "Cabell Farm" and "Piney Grove." Is was one of the few places where freed slaves could live in peace. Even though West Virginia was a Union state, many white residents of the valley despised Negroes. The 1870s newspapers tell of harassment such as beatings by mobs and petitions seeking to ban Negroes from the county.

In 1890, Congress passed a law saying certain benefits would be denied to states that didn't educate Negroes - so, in 1891, the West Virginia Legislature passed an act creating the "West Virginia Colored Institute." A site was sought, but several communities, including St. Albans, angrily rejected offers to become the home of the black institution.

Finally, according to John C. Harlan's History of West Virginia State College, Governor Aretas B. Fleming and his staff boarded a boat and chugged down Kanawha River looking for a site. At the Negro colony nine miles downriver, they were met by black residents who welcomed the idea.

Samuel Cabell's daughter Marina sold the state a 30-acre tract for $2,250, and other lots gradually were purchased until an 80-acre campus was acquired. (Marina became postmaster of the town, and was said to be the first Negro woman in the United States to hold such a position.)

The town was named Institute, and kept the name even though the "Colored Institute" later was given other titles and finally evolved into West Virginia State College.

Mary Barnes Cabell died in 1900, an 85-year-old great-grandmother revered by her clan. She was buried in a little family cemetery alongside her slain mate. His tombstone, already weathered by then, indicates he was 63 years old when he was killed, and it spells his name

"Cabble," one of the pre-Civil War variants of the name. Two of their daughters are buried in the same cemetery.

Many of the descendants have dispersed, but two granddaughters - Miss Ruth Holt Cabell and Mrs. Gwen Carter - still live in Institute, as do a number of great-grandchildren.

Today's Institute is a jam-packed academic and industrial center. In addition to the college, it has the Carbide chemical plant, the dormant Goodrich-Gulf plant, the state vocational rehabilitation center, the state police training academy, and a couple of hundred homes that have become racially integrated with scattered white occupants.

Hardly noticed in the bustle is the final refuge of the two people who started it all. The little Cabell Cemetery has been surrounded by the buildings and driveways of the vocational rehabilitation center. A lone tree bends over the graves of the murdered plantation owner and his beloved former slave woman.

*A paper read at the annual meeting of the West Virginia State Historical Society, Charleston, October 3, 1970.

TRUE STORIES OF THE HORRORS OF SLAVERY

Charity Anderson – Ex-Slave

Interview with Charity Anderson in approx. 1936

Volume I

Alabama Narratives

Charity Anderson

Interview with Charity Anderson

—Ila B. Prine

Charity Anderson, who believes she is 101 years old, was born at Bell's Landing on the Alabama River, where her owner, Leslie Johnson, operated a wood-yard, which supplied fuel to the river steamers, and a tavern where travelers whiled away the delays of a dubious riverboat schedule.

Rheumatic and weak, she no longer ventures from her house in Toulminville, on the outskirts of Mobile, but sits, with her turbaned head and bespectacled eyes, rocking the long hours away in a creaky old chair and knitting or sewing, or just gazing into a past painted by the crackling flames in the fireplace.

"I has so much trouble gittin' up and down de steps and ober de groun', I jist makes myself happy heah, cause—thank de Lawd—I'se on Zion's March," is her resigned comment.

"Missy, peoples don't live now; and niggers ain't got no manners, and doan' know nothin' 'bout waitin' on folks. I kin remember de days w'en I was one of de house servants. Dere was six of us in de ole Massa's house—me, Sarai, Lou, Hester, Jerry and Joe. Us did'n' know nothin' but good times den. My job was lookin' atter de corner table whar nothin' but de desserts set. Joe and Jerry, dey was de table boys. Dey neber tetched nothin' wid dere han's, but used de waiter to pass things wid.

"My ole Massa was a good man. He treated all his slaves kind, and took good kere of 'em. But, honey, all de white folks wan't good to dere slaves. I's seen po' niggers 'mos' tore up by dogs and whupped 'tell dey bled w'en dey did'n' do lak de white folks say. But, thank de Lawd, I had good white folks and dey sho' did trus' me, too. I had charge of all de keys to de house, and I waited on de Missis' and de chillun. I laid out all de clo'se on Sat'dy night, and den Sunday mawnin's I'd pick up all de dirty things. Dey did'n' have a thing to do. Us house servants had a hahd job keepin' de pickaninnies out'er de dinin' room whar ole Massa et, cause w'en dey would slip in and stan' by his cheer, w'en he finished eatin' he would fix a plate for 'em and let 'em set on the hearth.

"No mam, Missy, I ain't neber worked in de fields. Ole Massa he neber planted no cotton, and I ain't seen none planted 'tell after I was free. But, honey, I could sho 'nuff wash, iron and knit and weave. Sometimes I weaved six or seven yahds of cloth, and do my house work too. I lernt the chillun how to weave, and wash, and iron, and knit too, and I's waited on de fo'th generation of our fambly. I jes' wish I could tell dese young chillun how to do. Iffen dey would only suffer me to talk to dem, I'd tell dem to be more 'spectful to dere mammies and to dere white folks and say 'yes mam' and 'no mam', instid of 'yes' and 'no' lek dey do now.

"All dis generation thinks of is 'musement. I neber had seen a show in my whole life 'tell jes' dis pas' yeah when one of dem carnival things wid de swings, and lights, and all de doin's dey have stop right in front of our house heah.

"And I ain't neber been in no trouble in all my life—ain't been in no lawsuits, and ain't been no witness eben. I allus treat ebrybody as good as I kin, and I uses my manners as good as I knows how, and de Lawd sho' has took good keer of me. Why, w'en my house burnt up, de white folks helped me so dat in no time you couldn't tell I ebber los' a thing.

"But, honey, de good ole days is now gone foreber. De ole days was railly de good times. How I wish I could go back to de days w'en we lived at Johnson's landing on de riber, when de folks would come to ketch de steamboats and we neber knowed how many to put on breakfas', dinner or supper fo', cause de boats mought be behin' times. I ain't neber had to pay a fare to ride a steamboat needer. I was a good lookin' yaller gal in dem days and rid free wherever I wanted to go.

"But whut's de use dreamin' 'bout de ole times? Dey's gone, and de world is gettin' wicked'er and wicked'er, sin grows bolder and bolder, and 'ligion colder and colder."